Reflections on Friends, Comrades & Heroes

Other titles

Reflections on Industry and Economy
Reflections on Media and Gender Issues
Reflections on Good Governance and Democracy
Reflections on Labour and Trade Unions
Reflections on Africa and Global Affairs

Reflections on Friends, Comrades & Heroes

Issa Aremu

malthouse MP

Malthouse Press Limited

Lagos, Benin, Ibadan, Jos, Port-Harcourt, Zaria

First published 2015
ISBN 978-978-53321-5-5

Malthouse Press Limited
43 Onitana Street, Off Stadium Hotel Road,
Off Western Avenue, Lagos Mainland
E-mail: malthouse_press@yahoo.com
malthouselagos@gmail.com
Tel: +234 (01) 0802 600 3203

"It is the dictate of history to bring to the fore the kind of leaders who see the moment, who cohere with the wishes and aspirations of the oppressed."

- *Nelson Mandela (1997 on Steve Biko's 20th Death Anniversary)*

Preface

Friends and friendships we make, drop and retain from childhood days, right through formal schooling at various levels, no matter how limited, to active work life and post-formal employment and then twilight years of life, form critical part of our lives. Some of them have undoubtedly left their mark, directly and indirectly on one, just as some persons from far and wide, and across the ages, have through their observed conduct and ideas and ideals somehow managed to form part of one's frame of reference in our uncertain journey through life.

In no particular order, neither of time or geography, I present in this book a few individuals whose paths I have been fortunate to cross, some whose infectious ideas and lives have been exceptional, comprising by most humane and human standards, worthy examples for emulation, and some others still who have such brilliant minds and applied them to critical examination of the human condition, the African condition, and such varieties of socio-political and economic domination as manifested in more recent times. And then the few who used power wisely. Needless adding some of them need not know, for those who are still alive, nor did those of them who have passed on, know I exist.

For some of my contemporaries, the comradeship, the often lively discussions stretching into wee hours of the morning, the dash away from tears-inducing teargas during demonstrations and strike actions, the hurried meal in all manner places, and other shared challenges have created some bonds of friendship, empathy and identification with some ideals and thus mode of existence. I owe all a debt of gratitude.

Then, lastly, are those undoubtedly disagreeable fellow columnists and top bureaucrats/policy makers and self-indulgent legislators whose utterances and preferred policy options they attempt to ram through aggravate both intellect and the soul, thereby triggering commensurate responses some of which you read here; they helped configure a volatile industrial relations environment and, in some ways, broadened my horizon. I thank all.

Table of Contents

- Castro: Humour With Facts - **1**
- Essential Bala - **5**
- Essential Imoudu - **10**
- Political Economy Without Claude Ake - **14**
- Mandela's Moral Challenge - **18**
- The Essential Saraki: A Nostalgia - **21**
- Walter Sisulu Is Dead, Long Live Freedom - **25**
- Essential Shagari At 80 - **28**
- Long Live Okadigbo - **31**
- MCK and the End of History - **32**
- Grave Concerns - **34**
- Wole Soyinka- The Man Died Not - **37**
- Understanding Achebe - **40**
- Yasser Arafat: A Day After - **43**
- Sam Nujoma: A Stateman Is Born - **46**
- Return Of Walter Rodney - **49**
- Who Speaks For Nigeria After Bala Usman - **52**
- Alao-Aka Bashorun: Lessons In Patriotism - **55**
- Mugabe @ 80 - **58**
- Re-Inventing Walter Rodney - **61**
- In Celebration of Life - **65**
- Essential Mandela At 88 - **67**
- Ghana At 50: Nkrumah's Second Coming - **71**
- Mandela: Long Walk For Humanity - **75**
- Fela's Uncompleted Works - **78**
- Sunday Awoniyi: A Day After - **82**

- Gambari's Nation-Building Challenges - **86**
- Shehu Yar'Adua: Ten Years Later - **91**
- Mugabe As History - **95**
- Who Then Leads Like Nelson Mandela - **99**
- Reagan: Lest We Forget - **101**
- Essential Obama - **104**
- In Praise of Dr. Lasisi Osunde I - **109**
- In Praise of Dr. Lasisi Osunde II - **114**
- Tajudeen Abdulraheem: Tribute To Tributes - **117**
- Ageing Like Mandela - **121**
- Gani: Non-State Actor of All Times - **125**
- Justice Mustapha Akanbi: Private Citizen, Public Good - **131**
- Rimi: In Praise of Audacity - **134**
- Yar'Adua In Praise of Civility - **138**
- Yar'Adua: Farewell To Civility - **141**
- Mandela: Age And Ideas - **145**
- Hassan Sunmonu (@70) For Beginners - **149**
- Keeping Fit At Fifty - **154**
- Essential Fidel @ 85 - **157**
- Bishop Hassan Kukah; Witness To Ordination - **161**
- Worthy Honours; Yar'Adua And Professor Gambari - **164**
- Quotable Ojukwu - **167**
- Bade Onimode; Remembering The Afro-Optimist - **170**
- Ojukwu; Farewell To Arms - **174**
- The Essential Comrade Pascal Bafyau - **177**
- Mandela @ 94 - **181**
- Femi Falana: In Praise of Principles - **184**
- Patrick Ibrahim Yakowa: A Tribute - **187**
- Essential Oshiomhole @ 60 - **190**
- Olaitan Oyerinde: A Life Too Short - 193
- Mandela Is Dead, Long Live Madiba's Legacy! - **195**
- Nelson Mandela, The Day After - **198**
- Alao Aka-Bashorun: Pan African To The Core - **201**

- Tribute To Aloysius Morgan Anigbo - **204**
- Dora Akunyili: Tribute To A Worthy Regulator - **207**
- Olaitan Oyerinde: Blessed Are The Dead - **210**
- Dr. Jibrin Ibrahim@Sixty; Not By Politics Alone – **214**
- **Index - 217**

About the Author

Comrade Issa Obalowu Aremu, NPOM, mni was born in 1961 to the extended family of Mallam Mahmood Aremu and Hadjia Afusat Amoke of Alapata and Kasandubu compounds of Ilorin respectively. He attended Ansar Ud Deen primary school, Ijagbo. He had his secondary education at Ilorin Grammar School before moving to School of Basic Studies, Ahmadu Bello University, ABU, Zaria in 1977.

Issa's passion for organizing and activism started in the late 1970s and early 1980s, decades of progressive and radical ideas in ABU. He was an active member of ABU students' unionism and rose to become the Secretary General of the reputable radical Marxist-Leninist Movement for Progressive Nigeria (MPN). He was among the score of students' leaders repressed with expulsion by Ango Abdullahi Vice Chancellorship in 1981 at his final year. He eventually obtained his BSc (Hons) degree in Economics from University of Port Harcourt in 1985 with Second Class Upper. He has his Master degree in Labour and Development studies from the prestigious Institute for Social Studies (ISS), The Hague, The Netherlands, in 1991. He is an alumnus of George Meany Labour Centre, Maryland, Washington, USA (1987 and 2003). He joined the labour movement as the Head, Economic/Research department of Nigeria Labour Congress (NLC) between 1987 and 1989. He later moved to the National Union of Textile Garment and Tailoring Workers of Nigeria (NUTGTWN), a private sector affiliate union of NLC in 1989. After 20 years of active union carrier, he rose from an organizing Secretary to become the General Secretary of the union in March 2000. He took over as the General Secretary of the union from Comrade

Adams Oshiomhole mni, the Comrade governor of Edo State and two times former President of Nigeria Labour Congress (NLC).

Comrade Issa Aremu is currently one of the Vice-Presidents of the Nigeria Labour Congress (NLC). In 2013 In Johannesburg, South Africa, he was elected the Chairman, new IndustriALL Global Union, Africa Region with more than 50 million members in 165 countries with headquarters in Geneva, Switzerland making an Executive African Member of IndustriALL Global Union. Having attended Senior Executive Course 27 of the National Institute (mni) for Policy and Strategic Studies, Kuru, Jos in 2005, Comrade Issa Aremu is a Member of the National Institute.

In 2013 he was elected the Secretary-General of the Alumni Association of the National Institute for Policy & Strategy Studies, AANI.

He is currently the Chairman of the Interim Management Committee of First Guarantee Pension Limited and a member of the tripartite National Labour Advisory Committee (NLAC) made up of government, employers and trade unions. He also serves in the Board of Labour City Transport Service (LCTS). He is the Chairman, International Committee of Nigeria Labour Congress (NLC).

Comrade Issa Aremu, mni has served on the Board of Michael Imoudu National Institute of Labour Studies (MINILS) and Nigeria Social Insurance Trust Fund (NSITF). His contributions helped to reposition these institutions as leading labour market institutions in Nigeria. He had served on the tripartite Federal National Minimum Wage, in 2000 and 2010 and Petroleum Products Pricing Regulatory Committee in 2003 as well as tripartite committee on Revival of textile and Garment industry. He has led negotiations and signed hundreds of national collective agreements on salaries, allowances, gratuity and pensions of textile, garment and tailoring workers over the years.

A visible leading member of mass national actions on socio-political issues during the struggle for democracy and against military dictatorship in the 1980s and 1990s, Comrade Issa is a weekly columnist with Abuja-based, *Daily Trust* newspapers. His published works include; *The Social Relevance of Trade Unionism, The Crises of Pricing*

Petroleum Products in Nigeria, Collapse of Textile Industry in Nigeria: Implications for Employment and Poverty Eradication and Tears Not Enough.

Comrade Issa Aremu, mni was one of the labour delegates to the 2014 National Conference. He was the Deputy Chairman of the National Conference Committee on Civil Society, Labour, Youth and Sports. He is a strong activist and advocate on, Redistribution of national wealth, improved Productivity and Re-Industrialisation of Nigerian economy. Recipient of many distinguished awards and recognitions, the President of Nigeria, Dr. Goodluck Ebele Jonathan, GCFR, on August 21, 2014 in recognition of his contribution to national productivity improvement and consciousness conferred on him the National Productivity Order of Merit (NPOM) Award. He is married with children.

Castro Combines Humour with Facts

> "I meet people who I immediately know are going to die young. I see them all worked up, bitter, tense but that's not my case. I think that something that has been a great help in this is that I'm able to LET GO; that I have a sense of humour; that I can see the light side, the funny side and even the ridiculous side of things that happen. That has helped me to hold on..."

That was Fidel Castro in a rare interview granted 15 months ago to two Americans – Dr. Jeffrey Elliot and Congressman Marvin Dymally – explaining how his sense of humour had seen him through the ordeal of leading the US-blockaded Island of Cuba. In the interview, Castro discussed a wide ranging number of issues, including US allegations of Cuba-Columbia narcotics connection, leadership and leaders, the Third World debt problem, Apartheid, the arms race and Cuba's relations with the United States and the USSR.

The three-day interview is now in a book form, *Nothing can change the course of history*. The handy book shows 59-year old Castro as a most knowledgeable man of events and issues in his country, the Third World and the world at large. More than that, it throws more light on Castro's personality and his vision of the world.

> "Material goods do not motivate me. Money does not motivate me at all. The lust for glory, fame, prestige does not motivate me. I really think ideas motivate me", said Castro, echoing Cuba poet, Jose Martins words: "All the glory of the world fits into a kernel of corn."

For Castro, Jesus Christ and the Prophet Mohammed are the world's greatest leaders because "…each of them had a doctrine, founded a doctrine and was followed by multitudes…they were religious leaders but leaders nonetheless."

His assessment of leadership qualities are based on the requirements of different historical possibilities. "If George Washington had been born 50 years after Independence, he might have been unknown and the same hold true if he'd lived 50 years before it."

Fidel sees Indira Gandhi, Argentine-born Che Guevera and scores of French revolutionaries, America's Roosevelt, Lincoln and Jesse Jackson as great leaders. But Castro would not answer in the affirmative that he is a "leader", remarking that it is an "old theory that associates historical events with individuals, and more so in the Third World where Western stereotype has equated "leader" with a "chieftain":

> "I am amazed that in West, where you suppose that there are cultured societies and that people think, there's such a strong tendency to associate historical events with individuals and to magnify the role of individuals. I can see it myself: Castro's Cuba, Castro did this, Castro undid that. Almost everything in this country is attributed to Castro, Castro's doing, Castro's perversities. That type of mentality abounds in the West, unfortunately, it's quite widespread. It seems to me to be erroneous approach to historical and political events."

Castro does not conceal his faith in human beings saying the potential capacity of human mind is infinite. "It is said that people use only 5 to 6 per cent of their mental capacity. (There are scientists who are doing research on this). Nobody can imagine the kind of computer a man has in his head." If there are "leaders" at all in Cuba, they are doctors, manual and intellectual workers, school teachers and students, all armed militia and "the legion of anonymous heroes who constitute the people."

Castro disagrees that he is a "masterful communicator" and humorously adds: "I have a great competitor and that's Reagan. Castro addressed the UN General Assembly for 4½ hours in September 1960 and often speaks for hours on end at rallies attended by millions of Cubans. "I have a stage fright," says Castro, who scorns written speeches, which he describes as always colder and often the fruits of abstract inspiration." "When you're in direct contact with the public nothing is artificial, nothing is abstract, you get better ideas, words are more persuasive, more convincing."

A striking feature of Castro's personality is his exceptional mastery of data and basic information to buttress logical analyses. He could forget telephone numbers, "unless there's a special motivation." "However, if you give me a figure on economics, I hear it or read it once and I don't forget. If you give me a figure on public health, on education, on economic programmes, or even scientific data, I don't forget."

Castro says, he has read Darwin's down to Alex Harley's *Roots*. He describes "Roots" as "a wonderful reconstruction of the human tragedy that was slavery." He has read the communist manifesto and classic works of Marx, Engels and Lenin down to Churchill's memoirs and anything published on Cuba that "I can lay hands on." He told his interviewers: "I can grab a book and forget you."

Fidel is virtually obsessed with the debt problem of Third World countries and he has only one answer for the debtors – "Don't pay." He compares the debt burden "to that torment in Greek mythology in which a man is doomed to push a large stone uphill for all eternity, a stone that always rolls down again before reaching the top." Debtors, he says, don't need new loans. Reason? "If Brazil is paying $12 billion a year for the interest on its debts, it doesn't need any loans; if it invested that $12 billion, it would have $120 billion for development purposes in ten years.

Mexico with great restrictions is exporting $23.5 billion worth of products and importing only $10 billion worth. It could invest more than $10 billion a year instead of paying interest on its debts. That makes over $100 billion in ten years. If Argentina is paying $5 billion, that would amount to $50 billion in ten years." Debtor, he maintains need not fear reprisals if they refuse to pay, since creditor countries need the former's raw materials:

> "Can you imagine an industrialized society - Switzerland, England, France, Spain, Italy, Western Germany, and the United States – without chocolate? Can you imagine those countries without coffee, tea or cashew nuts to go with their drinks? Can you imagine them without nutmeg, cloves, other spices, peanuts, sesame seeds,

pineapples, coconuts or coconut oil, for their mild and fragrant soaps?"

It is not bad faith says Castro, to repudiate the debt, especially as some faiths, Islam, for instance says "charging interest constitute robbery", while Christianity does not allow prohibitive interest rates.

In any case, Castro explains, parts of the accumulated debts only went for military spending, a part squandered, some siphoned to foreign accounts by ruling elites and a part stolen. Another returned to creditors: as flight of capital", little for "development".

Fidel is no longer desperate to normalise relations with the United States, since relations with socialist countries are more just and, reciprocal. "Don't swap a cow for a goat," says Castro, invoking an old Cuban saying. Castro would not discuss his private life but insists "with my private life…no problems". "I've always been allergic to social columns; to publicity about the private life of public men. I believe that's part of the few intimacies that one has."

Essential Bala

Perhaps the death of the then 36-year old Ntem Kuguwai of ABU, Zaria in 1983 on his way to Kashim Ibrahim Library, Dr. Mahmood Tukur and Claude Ake in 1996 in ADC air crash compared with Bala's in its suddenness, agony and cost to the already depressed and depleting Nigerian and African progressive community. The legendary liberation fighter, Amilcal Cabral of Guinea Bissau in 1992, in paying homage to late Kwame Nkrumah of Ghana, urged that 'our tears' should not 'drown the truth' about what Nkrumah stood for. Bala was certainly not Nkrumah. Yours sincerely is no Cabral either. These two great African revolutionaries among others however served as powerful sources of inspiration to us all during our nascent quest for social justice and fairness. In other words, bringing to the fore the essential world outlook and practices of Bala even amidst tears remains a worthy tribute to him and enduring legacy for future generation.

Essential Bala is pan-Africanism. Socialism and communism and the noise-level these ideologies elicited were often attributed to campus comrades in the 1980s. The truth however is that we knew of Nkrumah, Lumumba, Cabral, Garvey, Gadaffi, Fanon, Rodney, Kaunda, Dedan Kimatti, Mandela, Mugabe, Zik, Mokwugo Okoye, Raji Abdallah, Sa'ad Zungur, Mallam Aminu Kano and Murtala Mohammed well before Marx, Lenin, Stalin, Mao or Castro.

OAU just metamorphosed into African Union (AU). But, whence the African unionists? Bala's death on the eve of formation of AU is one significant African unionist denied. It is debatable if the bureaucrats of our Ministry of Integration and Co-operation would find useful his pan-African perspective and praxis, were he alive. Official non-recognition (expectedly), however does not in the least diminish a worthy comrade. On the contrary, daily incomprehension blurred vision and incoherence of our diplomats from Abuja to Lusaka about the objectives and orientation of the new African Union further stresses the real and potential loss that is Bala's death.

Pan-Africanism a la Bala is one heritage traceable to the great dreams of Marcus Garvey to unite all blacks against slavery, colonialism and discrimination. Pan African awareness was rekindled in us, thanks to African history, African literature and world history at the old SBS, ABU in late 1970s. These courses, ably taught by great instructors like Bala Usman, Ayo Olukotun, Obaloto, American history-scholar Bob Manuel among others, promoted consciousness about deplorable African conditions of colonialism, neo-colonialism, racism and Apartheid. This awareness motivated us to realise that the continent needed continent-wide mass actions against vestiges of colonialism, under-development and Apartheid. For Bala, African unity or African union could not have been another aping fad modelled after European Union (EU) as African diplomats are currently making us to believe. Nor was it another top-down 'African initiative' to be beggarly sold to G-8 group of rich nations. Rather, the imperatives of continental unity and union for Bala lie in the conditions of Africa itself.

Notwithstanding, the smear campaign against him by the Western politicians and media alike perhaps only Libyan Gadaffi's current version of African Union approximates Bala's. This great vision means that the abysmal conditions on the continent demand forging alliances with progressive forces of change, such that its diverse peoples would not further fall prey to predatory forces of oppression, exploitation, racism and in recent time wars and globalisation. Whether Bala's pan-Africanism would impact on the current soulless efforts at African Union would further put to test the continent's sense of appreciation of its great citizens. Given the current loss of memory, as it were, expressed depressingly in a historical approach to development and the casual manner with which we have abandoned the thoughts and deeds of the likes of Nkrumah, Lumumba and Cabral, it requires new compatriots to realise the dream of African citizen Bala.

The thirst and the search for egalitarian ideas of equality, equity and justice propelled Jibril and his comrades to socialism and communism. Thanks to the competent tutorship of great radical scholars like Yusuf Bangura, Rauf Mustapha, Jibo Ibrahim, Bjorn Beckman, late Ntem Kuguwai, late Tukur Mahmood, Bala Usman, Sidiq Abubakar, all of the great Faculty of Art and Social Science (FASS). Deafening collapse of socialism in the former Eastern European countries and the enthronement of global market dogma inadvertently makes identification with socialism an anathema.

Considerable erstwhile Leftists are now proud members of donor-given 'Right community' taunting 'pro-democracy' credentials to match. Whatever happened then to socialism? Comrades opt for 'human rights', almost without corresponding responsibilities in a continent begging for both rights and duties. Not few comrades proclaim end of ideology, altogether. Some actually became propagandists and apologists of military dictatorships of all traits. Some are simply miserable chieftains of ethnicity and regionalism, generating more heat and less light for our peoples seeking justice and development.

In contrast, Bala was un-apologetically a socialist, patriot and internationalist in Leninist non-doctrinaire sense of the word to the end. Any attempt to recruit Bala into ever unhelpful boring regional and ethnic tom beat must be seen for what it is – unconscious post humour disservice. Bala needs not 'redefine the national question' for he knows that it is an integral part of class and social relations and he shares this not 'hitherto' but all the time. This is understandable, given that commitment to socialism is conviction than a passing fad for him. He significantly also sees Marxism as a method and analytical tool and not a doctrine or prophesy.

Bala's capacity for analysis was self-evident in our under-graduate days such that it was clear that if he was unable to make a revolution, he would naturally end up a lecturer teaching revolution. He was adjudged a successful mass communication lecturer that turned out equally successful students in significant number. He will always be remembered for his erudite participation in Nigeria Television Authority (NTA) weekly media review produced by the legendary late James Audu. Nothing could be more revolutionary, blending theory and practice, refusing to be consigned to the margin and insisting to be in the mainstream.

This, points to another essential attribute of Bala – scholarship. Much has been said about the mass expulsion in ABU under the authoritarian vice chancellorship of Ango Abdullahi in 1981. Apart from the repressive character of the unprecedented expulsion aimed at weeding out the progressive forces on the campus, that singularly deployed big stick was meant to terminate budding inquiring minds, Bala's inclusive.

Remarkably, Bala turned his expulsion at final year into even greater search for knowledge and not despair as preferred by the inquisitor, thanks to his industry and exceptional hard work. He started and completed first, second and doctorate degree in unprecedented quick successions. The mediocre and failed radical is not Bala's. Failure is alien to him. On the contrary, excellence and distinction are hallmarks of genuine comrades, very well in the traditions of acknowledged radical thinkers and practitioners.

Undaunted, Bala returned to ABU and made the point that denial of first degree on trumped-up charges was only a calling to doctorate pursuits and not to slide into ignorance from which he chose to escape from in the first instance. Even when some renegade lecturer-supervisors brought subterfuge to undermine him, he resolved to leave his foot imprint on scholarship. Bala saw the bigger pictures in life, while his oppressors are pre-occupied with a mundane paltry obstacle building.

Paradoxically, Bala's fertile mind was nurtured in the functioning public primary and secondary schools in post-colonial Nigeria. This great mind was further watered in the vibrant public university system of 1970s and 1980s. Today, we shamelessly pay lip service to Universal Basic Education (UBE), pitch basic education against university education as if they are mutually exclusive, endlessly play politics with primary teachers' pay and ultimately destroy university education. Reproducing Balas (assuming it is possible) puts to test the sincerity of purpose of all our education administrators. When will there be public hearings on our collapsed public schools?

Few, at such tender age devoted so much time and energy to organisation building. 'Civil society' is the new fad generously being promoted by international financial institutions and 'development' agencies, following frustration with state-building they ironically promoted and funded in post colonial Africa. At a time it was far from being popular, Bala and his compatriots had realised the fact that Africa's future lies in vibrant civil society. This realisation flows from Claude Ake's observation that "people must 'own' their own development which means that they have to be its agents as well as its means and ends." Bala selflessly contributed to building or organisations that include students' unions, Movement for Progressive Nigeria (MPN), NUNS/NANS, Patriotic Youth Movement (PYMN), Academic Staff Union of Universities (ASUU), and CAPP, etc. For a country that is democratising without political parties, a country in which individuals and not programmes and organisations are in the contest for power, even without discernible differences in terms of ideas and vision, Bala's legacy in organisation-building around idea and issues is worth exploring even after death.

Bala is dead, Long Live Bala.

Essential Imoudu*

Assuming there is any theory and practices of unionism and unionists known as Imouduism, one significant variant of it must deal with longevity. At 100 this week, Pa Michael Aithokhaimien Imoudu upturns conventional wisdom about what actually promotes long-life. The labour icon has astonishingly combined stress, tension, agitation, deprivations and harassment that characterised his historic union life, with a century-long, long life. Imoudu's proves an exception to the latest UNDP typical report that once again puts Nigeria's life expectancy at 55. Pundits on struggling life definitely have a lot to reflect on in Imoudu's life. Himself an ideologue of Maoist leaning, Imoudu outlived Chairman Mao (82) and even his older successor, Deng Xiaoping (92). A convinced and proud Zikist (the first Nigeria Labour Congress (NLC) under his leadership in 1950, amidst controversy, affiliated to Zik's NCNC), Imoudu nonetheless outlived Zik. In 1987, he attended the funeral of Chief Obafemi Awolowo, his later years' benefactor, without extra support than his legendary walking stick. Interestingly the cited mentors and compatriots of Imoudu are themselves some case studies in longevity.

What has age then got to do with some 'icon-men' whose vocation is service to humanity? We all know that some men and women with deep impact on mankind often live shortened lives. But why do some of the world's struggling men turn some exceptions? Why do they not fall easy prey to those common afflictions that have shortened the lives of even the most affluent and comfortable that lay no claim to any greater human cause? Imoudu's life particularly assumes a mystique given that his notable contemporaries and

* Original text of this article was written in 1997 when Imoudu was 95

comrades in trade union movement have also long passed on. Witness, Alhaji H.P. Adebola, Gogo Nzeribe, Simeon Adebo, Wahab Goodluck, Odeyemi, Adio Moses, Armstrong Ogbonna, Mpamugo to mention but few. Pa Imoudu truly stands out as the mystery comrade, a senior '*Abami-Eda*' of trade union movement.

If longevity is an issue in Imouduism, unprecedented honesty of purpose and commitment to the road freely chosen is another variant of it. The road chosen leads to restoration of dignity of labour and upliftment of working men from the deprivations of wage-slavery particularly under colonialism. This honesty of purpose explains the exemplary spirit of self-sacrifice, spontaneity, firmness, courage and even naivety that were traits of Imoudu's active years. Roger Grail (1985) observes that since early 1930s when he challenged the absolute colonial labour regime in a strike, Imoudu became the "*bete noire*" of the colonial government adding that no other employee in Nigeria had more queries in his sacrifices, Imoudu intermittently went in and out of prisons and ended up indeed as a dismissed staff of Nigerian Railway without a pension. Only Hassan Sumonu, Frank Kokori and Adams Oshiomhole have demonstrated this sense of exceptional commitment since Imoudu's days.

There are weighty objective conditions that will always limit the actions of those who desire some changes in society. Imouduism however shows that the potentials always exist for these concerned men and women to act in ways and manners in which changes are inevitable. The existing order may not be altered, but it can be modified for the better. Imouduism emerged during depressions/inter-war years of (1919-1939). Starvation wages and casual labour and 'king-kong', industrial relations were the norms. Unions' functionaries were criminalised while colonial managers encouraged discriminatory/racist labour practices. Imoudu belongs to the first generation of Nigerian's work force. Together with his compatriots, they came in confrontation with the colonial order. The tactics and strategies were as diverse as the problems; strikes, rallies, appeal and petition writings. The only thing constant in Imouduism is the purpose: get justice for working men. It is to Imoudu's credit that the early struggles of workers humbled colonial employees, making them to reckon with labour and unions. The introduction of Cost of

Living Allowance (COLA) (modern day fringe benefits), abolition of casual labour, job-classification and minimum wage were the fallouts of the principled struggle of Imoudu's era. The subsequent labour reforms which made government to recognised unions through the famous trade union Ordinance of 1938, conscious official encouragement of enlightened union officials, strong and independent unions, mediation and conciliation in trade disputes, work men compensation legislation were logical outcomes of Imouduism.

Imouduism is also about organisation, the obvious foundation for workers' collective actions. In 1932, as a machinist, with other daily paid operatives and apprentices in Railway mechanical workshops, he formed the then Nigerian Railways workers' union, disregarding the then existing National Staff Union and the Mechanic Union, which represented only the elitist clerical/technical and compliment staff. Since then, Imoudu had been part of the formation of not less than ten unions and labour centres. He could disagree on principles and walk out of organisation, as was the case during the ideological acrimony of 1950s an 1960s, but only to form another organisation and not retreat to resignation. What is common to all Imoudu's led organisations is their Independence and democratic methods. Imouduism is an epitome of active and worthy voluntarism in which unionists relevance is measurable only (and only) in reference to workers interest and nothing more. As an organisation man, no restriction for Imouduism: started as an employee of Railways, Imoudu transformed into full time unionist spanning four decades. The artificial divide of "card/non-card" carrying is alien to Imouduism. Again few unionists have been able to cross all trade union bridges as the legendary Imoudu.

Lastly, Imouduism threw up men and (women mostly as supporters and sympathizers) all humble background representing the great diversities of great Nigeria. They were primarily motivated by the need of serve humanity through deep commitment to workers' union struggle. They included great names like Nduka Eze, I.O. Elias, Gogo Nzeribe, Mallam Nock, Ikoro, Uche Onu, Kaltungo, H.P. Adebola Simon Adebo, Etim Bassey, and Wahab Goodluck among others. These men found themselves playing the vanguard roles not by some design of their own. If you like, they just find themselves in position of leadership. Thanks to their honesty of purpose and learning by action. The result was the laying of foundation for one of the pillars of post-Independence namely: trade union movement. Nigeria's political parties actually learn from the wealth of experience generated by these pioneer unionists in organisation building, conduct of meetings and methods of strategy. It is significant to not that future leaders of post-independent Nigerian emerged from the rank of these self-made men. The notable include late T. Elias, a member of executive council of Railway Native Staff union in 1919. He later became a Professor of Law and President of the World Court in The Hague. Then late Chief Simon Adebo, he was the secretary to Federal Union of Railway men under Imoudu leadership. He later became secretary to Western State Government and Nigeria's Ambassador to United Nations.

Yet it is the mystique of Pa Imoudu that he holds on to unionism until retirement. He resisted the lure of 'higher' life, which in turn underscores essential Imouduism. At a time the battle for 'higher' life (i.e. political offices) has assumed a frightening dimension (witness assassination, impeachment) Imoudu's humble but dignified self-contentment is a lesson for the few that care. We have rewarded national honours. When are we going to properly honour dignity of labour that Imoudu symbolises? Imouduism means disinterestedness of exceptional bent; once a unionist, always a unionist. This then explains why yours sincerely joins others today to wish Dr. Pa Imoudu a disinterred birthday at his Ora residence (not London) near Auchi.

Political Economy without Claude Ake

November passes for a special month in the calendar of political economy. Claude Ake died in the tragic ADC airline disaster in November 1997. It is not an exaggeration to say political economy as a tool for explaining socio-economic dynamics of Africa almost 'died' with the political economist himself. Since the tragic deaths of the likes of Amilcal Cabral, Ruth First, Fanon and Walter Rodney, never has Africa lost an enthusiastic spokesman and intellectual advocate. Yours sincerely was a privileged witness to one-man intellectual guerrilla was successfully prosecuted by late Ake in defence of Africa.

It was during the occasion of an historic international conference on *Rethinking Emancipation Concepts* in 1991 by the prestigious International Institute of Social Studies, ISS, The Hague, Netherlands.

By consistent presentations Africa and indeed Asia had emerged at this historic conference as foot-notes in the evolution of emancipatory ideas and actions. In particular, Africa was presented as a burden with dubious distinction in senseless war, famine, under-development, poverty and disease. Ake's intervention at this conference, albeit on the last day, offered a food for thought, for a largely Euro-centric menu packaged as international conference to the prevailing myth that China was known to the world through the Tienammien-Square students' riots and the attendant Chinese authorities' clampdown. Ake raised an exceptional objection.

In his characteristic lady-like, soft-voice that belied his ever-entrenched resolve, Claude insisted it was intellectual lip-service of Euro-centric bent that would 'discover' China through Tienammien-Square. According to him, with a billion populations, China was actually the world that needed no discovery, certainly not through a storm in a tea cup like a students' protest. On Africa, Ake observed that the celebrated stories of despair, repression, wars, famine and bizarre are mainly from the formal structures of states that are in themselves legacies of slavery, brutal conquests and colonialism, structures that are still linked to the current global formal system of exploitation and oppression.

He maintained that success stories abound in non-visible, non-formal interactive communities of the continent, which according to him, engenders harmony, peace, entrepreneurship, shared values, fairness and justice and even gender equality. Ake was unapologetically romantic about Africa's non-visible past. He actually presented Africa's unanimous heroes and unreported processes and presented a remarkable but courageous outing in a setting many "African" scholars sought acceptance through slavish compliance with received wisdom.

After his triumphant presentation at this historic conference even at the risk of being smeared as an apologist of Africa's failed states, Ake shared his frustration with me. He said it was paradox that notwithstanding the advocacy for a worthy continent, governments and their agents back home still hounded his likes, treating them with suspicion. That Ake died in a mysterious and suspicious crash confirmed his genuine fear.

Five years after, the question is: how has African political economy fared? Ake died on the note of despair and incredible optimism. On despair, the master of sharp words in the tradition of radical scholarship deployed the worst of epigrams and aphorisms to depict abysmal continental reality. Two years before his death in 1995, he was categorical and insisted that: "Most Africa is not developing. Three decades of effort have yielded largely stagnation, repression or worse. The tragic consequences of this are increasingly clear: a risking tide of poverty, decaying public utilities and collapsing infrastructure and social tensions and political turmoil, and now, premonitions of inevitable drift into and violence." He wrote of "spectre of encircling chaos", observing that conflict has turned Africa into a continent of refugees and displaced persons. About six million of the world's estimated refugee population of 17 million are Africans and approximately 15 million of the 25 million internally displaced people worldwide are Africans.

When today, we consider the degeneration of hitherto "stable" states like Ivory Coast into lawlessness and continuous blood-letting in Liberia, self-inflicted "political", 'communal'/'religions' violence in many parts of Nigerian almost apocalyptic vision of Ake turned prophetic. Not to mention the perpetual statelessness of Somalia, attrition in the Congo and Central African Republic. Since his eternal exit more grim statistics have been rolled out from the despair mill. For instance, according to the World Bank,

> "of the world's six billion people, 2.8 billion (almost half) live on less than $2 a day and 1.2 billion (1/5) live on less that $1 a day; of the 1.2 billion living on $1 a day, 23.3 per cent live in sub-Saharan Africa, the second worst region to South Asia. In Nigeria, 80 million (2/3) of population are said to be poor."

Even more worrisome to Ake was that in spite of these problems, unlike elsewhere where crises promoted great ideas, in Africa – "no promising initiatives on the horizon." "There are not new redemptive ideas on the table, a state of affairs that is not helped by the ideological catholicity of the post-cold war world", he lamented. This singular worry about the current malaise, especially his questioning of the "very viability of Africa" made Ake vulnerable to accusation of Afro-pessimism. But Afro-pessimism was non-representative of Ake's position. He was a revolutionary preoccupied with development and transformation. To the extent that every revolutionary is an optimist, Ake dared not be accused of Afro-pessimism. Indeed, he stood and in intellectually pushed for Afro-optimism as indicated above.

The real tribute to Ake will be to acknowledge the emerging ray of hope, however marginal, in Africa's political economy. Since his death, it is refreshing that civil war ended in Sierra Leone and remarkably largely due to Africans' efforts with support of genuine friends in international community and civil societies. Of special significance is that Sierra Leone did peaceful transition from civilian to civilian government with active contestations by dozens of independent political parties, refuting the pessimism that civilians-to-civilian transition is impossible in the sub-region. Ghana recorded similar feat, pitting to rest the views of those who currently striving to change rules in Nigeria on account of so-called problem of second-term. If Sierra Leone emerging from war could transit, Nigeria should and must even do better in 2003.

On the economic front, since Ake's death, African statesmen (still no women) seemed to have woken up from their slumber. Through NEPAD with all its limitations, we are now witnessing activist developmentalist state, a radical departure from do-nothing laissez-faire that hitherto enthroned survival of the few wicked and the greedy at the expense of the hard-working, conscientious majority. How we make these marginal positive changes in the political economy sustainable depend oh how we heed Ake's eternal policy advice on development. He insisted that sustainable development is the one rooted in a vision that is "consensual." People, he said, must be made the means and ends of development so that they can own and defend the processes.

Lastly, he insisted that we strengthen state capacity and reject ideas that want to roll back state role in development. According to him,

> "Democratic development does not as is often assumed, mean suspicion of the state and undue restriction of the role of the state. A strong state is not an impediment to development, including democratic development. On the contrary it is an asset. What really matters is not whether the state leans towards interventionism or laissez-faire but the quality of its intervention."

Whether African statesmen and peoples will heed Ake's advice on development and democracy, time will tell. As a proud African of exceptional commitment, Ake can only be accused of excessive concern, not lack of it.

Mandela's Moral Challenge

US President George W. Bush "has no foresight" and "cannot think properly.' And that is official and authoritative. The authoritative verdict is that of Nobel Peace laureate and former South African President, Nelson Mandela. Perhaps there can be no such authority on foresight than Mandela himself who as far back as 1961 when others were blind to see it all, declared: "No power on earth can stop an oppressed people determined to win their freedom." His foresight and deep-seated resolve together with that of millions of other compatriots saw South African black people through the tyranny of Apartheid, notwithstanding his exceptional singular sacrifice of 27 years in prison. Bush can certainly ignore rhetoric from Iraq and North Korea to his own chosen warpath but he can only ignore this exceptional moral challenge from Mandela at his own moral peril and consequent political decline.

It is not just that the message comes from Madiba but precisely because true to most of his worthy interventions since retirement (without being tired) the latest from Mandela carries similar words of wisdom meant to rescue humanity from those bent on destroying it.

Take for instance Mandela's charge that Bush lacks foresight. Nothing could be more charitable because yours sincerely thinks that together with lack of foresight the President of the most powerful (not necessarily the most moral) country on earth also lacks benefit of hindsight. When Bush declared that regardless of UN and increasing ant-war global coalition, America would 'go it alone', it was clear that memory is in short memory in Washington. America and indeed any national cannot go it alone in our ever-interdependent world. It is not just about some brute force or brutal power but also about a painful reality that we all need each other after all. In late

August 2001, Bush and his arrogant and ignorant team ignored the world opinion and boycotted Durban UN Conference on Racism and Xenophobia on the account and assumption that America could go it alone and disregarded resolutions that were not favourable to its positions with regards to Israel and Palestine. It was a great paradox that a month after, in the wake of September 11-terror attack, America actually needed the world than the world needed it. All of a sudden, American unilateralism gave way to world multi-lateralism as the world rose in solidarity to condemn terrorism and joined US in solidarity and support with African inclusive. It is therefore not just lack of foresight on the part of current American leadership but also lack of retrospection on the part of its flag-bearer, George Bush, to say that it would go it alone on Iraq regardless of world opinion.

Mandela is perfectly right to say that no country has ever committed worse 'unspeakable atrocities' like America (remember 'constructive engagement' with Apartheid). However one should add that no country has ever benefited in human solidarity like America as the world came to its support following September 11 attack and for it to barely two years after, trample underfoot the feelings of this generous world amounts to a worst exhibition of ungratefulness and sheer ignorance. To this extent, Mandela's charge is a timely reminder to Washington that those who go alone must definitely grief alone. It is debatable if George H. Bush, Snr. had the benefit of tragic September 11 he would have ventured into Gulf War I in 1991 the way he did, which shows how America had inadvertently moved from bad to worse.

The great tragedy of Bush presidency is that it turns tested American friends into enemies thanks to what Mandela aptly observes as improper thinking and lack of foresight. Nelson himself is a good friend of America. He once had these generous remarks about USA. Addressing a joint session of the houses of Congress of USA in 1994, he said both USA and South Africa:

> "are linked by nature, but proud of each other by choice. The stand you took established the understanding among millions of our people that here we have friends, here we have fighters against racism who feel hurt because we are hurt, who seek our success because they too seek victory of democracy over tyranny."

But that was when USA had the President with foresight and clear thinking in the person of Bill Clinton. Today America not only lost good friend like Mandela but also allies like France and Germany which are distancing themselves from increasingly questionable position of Bush with respect to Iraq.

On the one hand we are told that the problem with Iraq is its refusal to cooperate with UN arms inspectors on its 'arms of mass destruction'. But the UN inspectors have accepted as much that Iraq has been cooperative and they (i.e. UN inspectors) should know better given the way they were rudely expelled by North Koreans on the same mission and of course given that they dare not venture to check Israel with similar arms stock piling. The American motives are certainly less altruistic than they present them. According to *African Business* of February 2003, "the real objectives of the Bush administration appear gaining direct access to 'black gold' rather saving the world from Iraq's potential chemical or biological weapons." According to the Pew Global Attitudes survey, chaired by Madeleine Albright, former US Secretary of State, some 70 per cent of French public believe the US's intentions are largely 'oil-motivated'. Iraq's proven reserves 115bn barrels – are almost four times greater than America's 30.4bn barrels. Tariq Aziz, Iraq Deputy Prime Minister bluntly put it: "The aim of US policies is the oil in the Gulf." True, conquering Iraq will present a tremendous gift for US oil majors likes of Exxon, Mobil and Chevron Texaco. The country's untapped oil resources are estimated at between 220-300bn barrels and potential output capacity could surge to 6-8m b/d within the medium-term given substantial foreign capital and technical inputs. The official opposition – Iraq National Congress would obviously grant exploration and development rights to US oil giants." Perhaps this truism explains lack of proper thinking on the part of Bush as aptly observed by Nelson Mandela. To be 'oil-motivated is to lack foresight as well as benefit of hindsight.

The Essential Saraki: a nostalgia

On May 17, 2003, *ThisDay* carried the most extensive interview so far then with the late Dr. Abubakar Olusola Saraki when he turned 70. What an anniversary copy for keep by those struggling to come to terms with the Saraki phenomenon in particular and Nigerian political leadership in general! Inspired by that singular historic interview I did a reflection entitled "Essential Saraki at 70". Some of the issues raised in that reflection remain valid today, albeit posthumously. Saraki, the man his people fondly called *Oloye*, had always been in the news in defence either of his abused political trust by scores of political associates or his often misunderstood political positions on topical national issues. That historic interview at 70 was refreshingly more in the affirmative and, (if you like) on the offensive to the extent that it laid bare essential thoughts and practices of Saraki, Waziri of Ilorin. Paradoxically, *ThisDay* almost betrayed the significance of a worthy job with his caption: "'How I Made My Son Governor".

I wrote then that a true caption of such a good job should be "Essential Saraki at 70". *ThisDay*'s caption once again puts the man in defence of what did not require any defence (going by holistic reading of this interview). At worst the caption further promoted the smear and stereotype about Turaki as another "godfather". Interestingly my friend and brother, Raheem Adedoyin, (who possibly should know better than me) also gave credence to this stereotype through his rather excellent but equally true-to-type/run-on-the-mill piece entitle "Quintessential Godfather at 70" in *ThisDay* May 17, 2003.

The essential Saraki is certainly *not* god-fatherism but servitude in the spirit and content of what the Almighty Allah enjoins all of us with knowledge and wealth (in- that- order of significance) should do to, others of lesser endowment. Contrary to false impression of a slave master presiding over a fiefdom, Saraki emerged as a defender of rights of all people to well being and well having, as far back as the 1960s as a young struggling young medical doctor. It was a combination of desire to serve patients at Lagos General Hospital casualty ward (at a time it was not popular to do so) and the genuine appreciation by the recipient-patients of his disinterested service (not money) that set Saraki on the path of public service.

I was a beneficiary of his generosity at a tender age as a secondary school student in Ilorin Grammar School in 1974. On a Friday, before Jummat, there was an instant hysteria, that late Waziri (then Turaki!) coming to Ilorin from Lagos wanted to see all the students. It was difficult to phantom how someone of *Turaki* standing would insist to see us the students of a public community school by the road side. But there he was admonishing us to take our education seriously after humbly introducing himself. His shared life experience with respect to primacy of education remains a lifelong constant reminder to some of us to excel in knowledge pursuit. Certainly *Oloye* caught us young!

We are all political animals after all. But how many a political animal would deliberately and disinterestedly serve people as *Waziri*? Saraki was not on government scholarship, yet he gave back more to the community than those who from cradle to grave live like leeches on the community. Perhaps the late *Bashorun* Abiola only compared with Saraki in a disinterested service to community. In a country in which most members of the political elite strive for what they could grab for self help in terms of money, properties and vain tittles, Saraki's almost singular anonymity in charity was legendary. He did impress on some of us as an accessible community man whose house in Ilorin is just another house in the neighbourhood. He was not a godfather, demanding roads or empty water tank be named after him. He was not breathing down on all through idolized billboards either. On the contrary he was a servant-leader of his people well before late Musa Yar'Adua popularised the servant-leadership type. When asked about what he would be remembered for Saraki was as unambiguous as he was in 1960s: "I will like to be remembered as that man who helped the sick get treated, the man who helped put a child in school, the man who helped that poor woman pick her life after losing so much in business or whatever. And think the chain will continue."

Later day political life of Saraki threw up scores of controversies and few conspiracy theories. However the bigger picture I saw was that of political disinterestedness rather than political dynasty.

Having supported the political mass movement that enthroned four governors in quick succession namely; Adamu Attah, Cornelius Adebayo, Shaba Lafiaji and Muhammed Lawal (three of whom are not from Ilorin emirate and none of whom is his relation), it is therefore politically uncharitable to slam Saraki with dynastic tendencies. Indeed thanks to *Oloye*'s political astuteness, it was easier for an Ebira man (Adamu Attah!) to be a governor in a bigger Kwara (inclusive of Kogi state) than he could possibly be today in a smaller Kogi. Many political "sons" or "daughters" of the late *Oloye* certainly abound!

Significant for me too is that Saraki was labour friendly. He was instrumental to the historic enactment of the first minimum wage Act of 1981 as a senate leader following the struggle of NLC led by Comrade Hassan Sunmonu. He was also instrumental to the establishment of Michael Imoudu Labour Institute in Ilorin, a fast growing centre of labour studies in Africa, an institute that eternally immortalizes Labour No 1, Michael Imoudu.

The essential Saraki's qualities are the twin issues of education and gender sensitivity. According to him, having been born into wealth, "education is very important. My father left me a lot of properties. But I have not touched them. It is the education I'm living on and the reason I sent my children to the best of schools in the world". Saraki shows that knowledge is wealth and that wealth is knowledge. In a country with new illiteracy, in which governance has not been knowledge-driven resulting into public poverty as different from public prosperity, it was quite refreshing to see one politician obsessed with education after Chief Obafemi Awolowo, the great education protagonist himself. Lastly, no politician has been so much concerned with the women's plight like Saraki, the *Oloye*. Indeed,

Saraki showed that if your support base was truly gender sensitive with considerable concern for those on the margins like the women, nobody can possibly stop you. He was truly a politician of the 'heart'. May Allah grant him eternal peaceful rest!

Walter Sisulu is Dead, Long Live Freedom

'His absence has carved a void. A part of me is gone'
- Nelson Mandela.

While we are muddling through the murky water of political partisanship, South Africa hit the headlines, albeit on two historic tragic-paradoxes. One was an irreparable loss, while the other is still redeemable, at least if we care and we are not hypocrites who shed tears for some and chuckle at some.

Walter Sisulu, an African patriot, 1964 Rivonia trial co-accused and anti Apartheid fighter, mentor and comrade of Nelson Mandela died last Tuesday at the age of 90. Week earlier, we had been confronted with the rude news of a jail-sentence of Winnie Mandela, irrepressible anti-Apartheid of equal significance, on alleged corruption charges. These are certainly separate development but a critical re-look shows that they are inseparable given that they are all minuses and NOT plus for Africa.

Of remarkable significance, is the post-humus assessment of Sisulu by the (Western) media. We are being told that what distinguishes Walter was his '*simplicity*' and '*humility*' as if others of his likes are '*naughty*' and '*immodest*'. We are further told he's survived by Albertina, his wife of 59 years, confirming his gentleman status. He actually reportedly died on his wife's lap, (*a remarkable feat in continent in which many a political leader reportedly packed up on you-know-whose lap*) The question that average African student, increasingly bereft of knowledge about the continent (*no-thanks to the closure of universities by the combined conspiracy of government and ASUU*) is; which kind of a system condemned such a gentleman to life imprisonment made to still spend 26 years of his adult life in prison? Why was he sentenced to life imprisonment in the first place? Put the other way round, why would we celebrate Sisulu's death, when in life we (read; *the West and its media*) for long, sustained and spiritedly defended the obnoxious system of Apartheid that made monster out of a gentleman like Walter Sisulu? The truth is that Sisulu's death once again underscores the imperative of freedom for humanity. We cannot genuinely mourn the death of this great son of Africa, if we pay lip-service to liberty, if we make freedom divisible (good for others, bad for some) and shamelessly persecute the likes of Winnie on, the altar of some conspiratorial charges as it was during the Apartheid days. Walter Sisulu's life showed that to gain freedom, one should renounce a gentleman status and prepare for enormous sacrifices that may conceal but not betray the inherent humility that Almighty Allah created us with. What legacy do we then remember Walter Sisulu for?

First is sacrifice. Even by South African standard, (everybody from an ordinary man to the priest was made to resist Apartheid), there is a consensus that no family was more dedicated to liberation than the Sisulus. In a continent in which families want to survive at the expense of others, selflessness of the Sisulus remains legendry. He cut short his studies on account of resistance to Apartheid. It was in Robin Island he completed his BA studies, making the point that nothing (not even Apartheid maximum jail house) could stop the mind bent on looking for knowledge. You can imprison the man, not his mind. The incarceration took a toll on Sisulu such that before he died, he could barely see. That the likes of Sisulus freely forgave (without forgetting) their jailers in spite of the arrogance of Apartheid chieftains to say sorry before the *Truth and Reconciliation Commission* underscores the sense of sacrifice of the Sisulus.

The second is courage and leadership. The man that discovered and encouraged Mandela needed no introduction in courage and leadership. Walter was perhaps more acknowledged than anybody in his (Mandela's) memoirs, *Long Walk To Freedom*. Either from the trenches, the prison or the presidency, the two passed through the 'valley of death'.

Thirdly is Sisulus' lesson in leadership and followership. Mandela acknowledged him as a mentor, with superior vision (*he rescued Nelson from the danger of reversed racism by, amidst sharp exchanges, insisting on all inclusive multi-racial struggles*). Yet he took a back stage to become a deputy to the same Mandela during the first ANC presidency. In a continent in which friendship and comradeship is under stress (*no thanks to selfishness*) and leaders and followers are at longer-heads, Sisulu is a great loss. African Union (AU) has truly lost a unionist.

Lastly was the abiding commitment to freedom. Freedom was a cause he was prepared to die for. During the Rivonia trial, before the racist hangman, he like Mandela courageously insisted on abolition of Apartheid.

It is this commitment to freedom that will outlive Sisulu. Our renewed commitment to this great legacy of Sisulu tests our true sense of loss. We cannot say we are mourning Sisulu, when Winnie Mandela remains as persecuted as it was under Apartheid. We have been told that her recent sentencing, which she rightly appeals underscores that nobody '*is above the law*'. Law? Remember that Mandela and Sisulu were jailed under the 'law'. Unjust law, selective law that vilifies, lionises, victimises Winnie (and Winnie alone) (*No known Apartheid criminals have been arraigned not to talk of being sentenced*) is as obnoxious as Apartheid law. We cannot mourn Sisulu and close our eyes to Winnie's ordeal. Sisulu is dead, long live freedom!

Essential Shagari At 80

The spectre of leadership hunts Nigeria. The literary giant, Chinua Achebe, was once categorical to say the problem with Nigeria was leadership. With benefits of history Achebe might be saying the truth but might not necessarily be privy to the whole truth. Nigeria is certainly not short of leaders but that is if we dare pay attention to history and details, less to lamentation.

Former President Shehu Shagari recently marked 80 years birthday. The national acknowledgement of the leadership qualities of the former President shows that the problem with Nigeria may not necessarily be absence of leadership but lack of acknowledgement of some worthy leadership qualities until we are overwhelmed with unworthy leadership prototypes.

One essential quality of Shagari is dignity and humbleness with power. In his autobiography, *Shehu Shagari; Beckoned To Serve*, citing the enormous powers vested in the Commander in Chief by 1979 construction, he observed that there '…is thus some truth in the view that the President's powers were considerable…such that most people tended to think that all I needed to get things done was simply to issue a command.' He however added that any President would prefer such simplistic exercise of power but the reality is that there are personal, intuitional and socoi-economic factors that constraint absolutist exercise of constitutional powers. Indeed Shagari noted that effective leadership is not in some King Kong's dispositions but in constructive cooperation with the legislature, 'one's own colleagues, staff and political party as well.' The truth is that subsequent leaders after Shagari carried on as if they had absolutist powers, as if colleagues don't matter (and with pointed military dictatorship), as if the nation does not matter.

The other important attribute of Shagari's leadership is his remarkable singular ability to acknowledge the efforts and contributions of predecessors even while he did not agree with some of their policies. For instance he unquestionably conceded credits to Obasanjo's administration for the '*foresight in starting steel plants*' even as the regime's Land Use Decree constrained Green revolution policy of his administration. In his words; 'the Obasanjo Administration did a good job in planning and constructing a modern sea-port at Tin Can Island' even as he had cause to reverse the regime's forced relocation of Abuja's inhabitants and Obasanjo's notorious policy of wage freeze. Thus Shagari shows that nothing was personal; give credit where it was due and then move on to govern based on your own policies. The truth of the matter is that this rare quality in governance as a continuity started and ended with Shagari as subsequent regimes undo all works (including good works) of their predecessors denying them credits they deserve attributing all that is good to themselves and by precedence, waiting to be discredited once they live office. To show that President Shagari decried vindictiveness in governance witness how he courageously took an exception to the 'arrogance and vindictiveness of the administration of President Ronald Reagan'. The latter denied Nigeria's US Cargo planes to airlift some communication equipments (in the wake 1983 NITEL fire) just because the 'Nigerian foreign Minister had previously publicly attacked the US foreign policy on Angola'. By the way the latter-day distortionist who presented late Ronald Reagan as friend of Africa should better ask Shagari who presided during Reagan years.

The most remarkable attribute of Shagari is horizontal and vertical consensus building and tolerance in a polity rooted in acrimony and mutual war of attrition. For instance, Shagari ably backed Lagos metro-line project notwithstanding that Governor Lateef Jakande was from the 'vicious' opposition party. He exercised considerable Presidential restraint in the face of provocation of the Oyo state government whose officials demolished NPN houses. Today there is considerable war of attrition between Federal and Lagos state government over issues which called for inter-governmental co-operation and solidarity calling to question the wisdom in official celebration of Shagari leadership without following his method.

Lastly remarkable was the labour dimension of Shagari administration. Interestingly, Shagari leadership shared same malaise with most Nigerian leadership which tended to see all trade unionists' actions as being '*politically motivated*' as if contested government policies are less politically motivated. What distinguished Shagari leadership was his power of delegation, persuasion and negotiation. He reached a number of agreements with labour over wide range of issues that included minimum wage review, car and leave allowances, provident fund and decent work in general. It is to the eternal credit of Shagari' tenure and his team (the notable being Alhaji Shehu Musa) that there was only one national strike which lasted one day during the second Republic dispensation. According to President Shehu Shagari, in '…one particular instance in March 1982 I personally intervened to stop a major strike threat.' Which Heads of State since Shagari have not personally provoked major strikes?

Long Live Okadigbo

Bertolt Brecht (1898-19560 once observed that "*who struggles can fail. Who doesn't struggle has already failed.*"

Whatever is said posthumously about the late Dr. Chuba Okadigbo, what cannot be denied of him is that he did struggle for worthy ideals such as democracy, justice and nationhood. And he did so at a time numerous lots were shamelessly enlisting in the ranks of sycophancy and sheer complacency in the face of increasing national decay. We can accuse Chuba of excessive concern but certainly not lack of concern for nation building. To the extent that he did struggle and what he struggled for (i.e. prosperous and democratic republic) is far from being realised, Chuba in idealistic sense is not dead as such, if only his comrades not only mourn but also continue where he stopped. There is no doubt the country has lost another great patriot on the eve of independence anniversary and at a time patriots were becoming endangered species. May his soul rest in peace.

MCK and the End of History[1]

Apart from leadership crisis, the bane of our underdevelopment is loss of profound memory. We are moving in vicious cycle, unable to build on the positive past but eager to repeat the negative steps of the past. This in large measure, is due to the unhelpful disconnects between the present and the past and even most times with the recent past too. MCK Ajuluchukwu was the last of the historians of nationalism, development and progress. The death of MCK at the age of 82 means the end of historical method in development discourse. History is defined as a '...seamless web linking past, present and future.' MCK participated in the great struggle for independence from the colonial predators. He witnessed post-colonial First Republic with its promise of hope and development rudely aborted by military predators. More than once, as a democratic activist, he was in the vanguard of attempts to restore democratic heritage. Helplessly he saw these efforts being scuttled. He died frustrated, lamenting how we are muddling through not linking past with present, putting future generation in jeopardy on the altar of greed, corruption and sheer insensitivity. MCK was history personified a true '...*web linking past, present and future.*' His exit means history denied and memory loss, more so when we realise that he was yet to finish his memoir for those who still care for reflections in the context of rat race for grab.

MCK's last interviews were celebration of historical method in development discourse. Witness him; '*The First Republic was run on purely selfless pattern*'. Can we say as much of the Fourth Republic when ministers pay millions for portfolios and quickly recoup once in office? Again MCK reminded us that:

[1] (Daily Trust, Monday 13th October 2003, pp. 6)

> Zik, the Sardauna, Aminu Kano, they had no money. Aminu Kano died and had only ₦2 in his account. I've been to his house in Kano, there was no easy chair...The Sardauna had so much power in those days that he could have easily said that the whole money in the treasury should be transferred to his house. But he did without money. Abubakar Tafawa Balewa was owing £19,000 to Barclay's bank, now Union Bank, when he died.'

What lesson can we learn from this MCK's historic insight in modesty, selflessness and good governance? Today governors and government officials whose places of birth are not easily identifiable on any map are reportedly competing to have choice properties and choice accounts at choice corners of Europe and America, even as they are shamelessly denying their citizens basic needs. Will they today in sympathy with the late MCK pause a bit and realise that what matters in the final analysis is the legacy for common wealth and not avarice in the service of self-aggrandizement? May Ajuluchukwu's soul rest in peace.

Grave Concerns

"There will be life after Mandela" – Mandela 'On His Death'

How the Comrades and Compatriots are dying? It is bad enough to write on the demise of anybody, but more painful to reflect on the eternal exit of your comrades. First, Dr. Jubril Bala, a lecturer at Department of Communication, University of Maiduguri died in a motor-accident on his way back to Maiduguri over two years ago. Progressive life has never been the same since Bala's exist. Huge vacuum created in terms of articulation, engaging friendship, progressive/scholarship advocacy and above all tested commitment to societal transformation and change remains huge. The historic memorial of Zaria honour of Bala consoled but never healed the grave wound inflicted by his death.

Among compatriots at Zaria Bala Memorial was Abubakar Jika of Bayero University, Kano. A year ago, Jika also died in a ghastly motor accident along Zaria-Kaduna road, bringing home the painful truth that only the potentially dead mourn the actually dead. Yours sincerely together with Jika had engaged in polemics (true to our radical idealism) about what Jubril Bala stood for at Zaria memorial, not knowing that we were inadvertedly projecting about our own lives and times also. Both editors of *Daily Trust* and *New Nigeria* Modibo Kawu and Mahmoud Jega had holistic tributes on Jika, tributes which aptly capture my reflections on this great compatriot. Last week, Sheriff Ujudud commendably kept alive the spirit of Jika, reminding us of the singular void, Jika's death created while reviewing last week's BUK memorial service in his honour.

Death has long been likened to robbery whose impact denies us our valuables. Never before has this emotional comparison had an appeal until the recent deaths in quick succession of comrades Abdulrahman Black Masa and Chris Abashi.

Black died on January 27th Tuesday 2004 in Lagos without notice of illness. A brother, comrade and colleague of nearly 30 years, Black's death was another minus in an increasingly endangered progressive camp. We were together during the New Year. He was actually expected in Kaduna for SALLAH from Lagos where he was an editor with *New Age* newspaper for our usual SALLAH rendezvous.

Black's death underscores another mystery of death. Together with Black, Late Jibril, Chom Bagu and Lamis Dikko, fell victims among others, of prevailing ABU authoritarianism in 1981 on account of our students' activism. Post-ABU adventure however united Black and me more than any comrade. We started our working career as journalists with *Triumph* newspaper in the 1980s. Since then, Black remained an activist journalist.

Perhaps no progressive chronicler had traversed scores of newspaper houses like Abdulrahman; from *Triumph* to the *Economist, Policy*, *Anchor* to *New Age.* Even while going-up as a managerial staff, he maintained a regular column pushing for alternative views. It is to the eternal singular credit of Abdulrahman as a journalist that he post-humusly wrote his column from the grave (as it were) on Thursday, 29th of February, three days after his death and paradoxically the day he was buried. That posthumus piece is a compulsory reading in appreciating his life and times. He took an exception to doctrinaire privatisation, which enriches the well-known few and impoverishes anonymous multitude of our people. The current review of privatisation exercise and the scandalous revelation of alleged insiders' dealings and alleged disappearance of proceeds further confirm the fears of Abdulrahman Black about privatisation.

Black will however be more acknowledged for his militant progressive students' union days to be President of ABU students' Union was a feat. To emerge with unprecedented popular votes amidst authority's meddlesomeness and some reactionary students' smear campaign was legendry. Black was so far the only President so honoured with Students' Union secretariat named after him: Abdulrahman Black Centre. Thanks to the insistence of appreciative students in defiance of the then official dictatorship. As his nickname implied he was an African to the core in the progressive tradition of Walter Rodney, Walter Susilu, Nelson Mandela, Patrick Wilmot, etc. Today's official sickening celebration of "white" farmers (as if farming is colour-bound) is a disservice to the memory of anti-Apartheid Black who among others maintained equality of races in all human endeavours including farming.

Like Black, Abashi's life shows that it is not how long but how eventful and the extent we touch others' lives for the better. In 1982 Abashi was the President of National Association of Nigeria Students (NANS). He eventually became the Chairman of Nasarawa Eggon Local Government Council where he applied theory of change to transform a hitherto backward council. He was also ANPP deputy gubernatorial candidate. Very few comrades had made such a remarkable impact in Establishment politics as Chris Abashi. Both Black and Chris are "minorities" but they decisively registered a majoritarian/international impact, making the point that it is not what we are ascribed by birth but what we can achieve through perseverance and commitment. The grave concerns are not that the comrades died but the challenge to continue where they stop. Mandela was asked about his death. His remark was characteristically optimistic; "*There will be life after Mandela*". Let the struggle continue after Black and Abashi. May their graves be spacious. (Amen)

Wole Soyinka: The Man Died Not

"What doesn't kill us makes us stronger" – *Moe;scje*

The Man Died not. On the contrary, the man actually survived uneven 70 years. Paradoxically, UNDP's recent report does not envisage Soyinka celebrating 60th not to talk of 70th birthday. Released on the eve of Nobel winner's birth-day, United National Development Programme (UNDP) ranks Nigeria 151 out of 171 in human development, marginally ahead of countries like Haiti (154) and Sierra Leone (171) and far below Cuba (52), Saudi Arabia (78), South Korea (28), Malaysia (60) and even Ghana (132). Central to UNDP's human development index are life expectancy, literacy and education levels, per-capital income and health care. Judging by UNDP's Nigeria rating of life expectancy at less than 50, literacy 50% and per-capital income of $500, Soyinka is truly an exception to the rule with abundant blessed bonuses worthy of celebration.

Essential Soyinka at 70 is survival where everything is short-lived including bank deposits and loans. How Soyinka survives these turbulent decades of Nigeria's boom, burst and doom remains as obscure as scores of his writings. Proverbial water has passed under Nigerian bridges since Soyinka wrote *The Man Died.* Soyinka's 1970s Nigerian man died of "spiritual kwashiorkor" because he kept "silent in the face of tyranny". In 2004, the boy dies before he actually grows into a man (no thanks to infant mortality and now AIDS). If however he survives infancy, he dies of want of jobs, insecurity of tenure, low wages, non payment of pensions, police accidental discharges, "religious crises", robbery, homelessness, road "accidents" and all that make up present day Nigerian malaise including silence. Ben Okri had long warned the poets to "be cunning" by learning some of the miracles of life which is survival. He must have undoubtedly inferred this from Soyinka's fruitful life. Steve Biko was not so lucky. He was murdered in his prison cell by Apartheid regime in 1977. Dele Giwa, a writer in his own right, was bombed the year Soyinka got Nobel Prize.

"Writers are dangerous when they tell the truth". "Writers are also dangerous when they tell lies" wrote Ben Okri. The strength of Soyinka, spanning decades, lies in his capacity to tell the truth at a time it was risky to do so. He was imprisoned for 2 years for daring to call for caution amidst hysteria and xenophobia during the civil war. His almost singular advocacy against military dictatorship is well acknowledged. In recent time, at the risk of blackmail, he demanded for justice for the slain Justice Minister, Bola Ige and insisted on defense of Nigeria's Bill of Rights amidst the heat and fume of tear-gas.

Soyinka can be rightly accused of excessive concerns about African development bordering on playing to the gallery. But no one dares accuse him of indifference, complicity in decay that is fastly defined as Nigerian project. This trademark, he shares with late Aminu Kano, Claude Ake, Gani Fawehinmi, Balarabe Musa, Abubakar Umar and Adams Oshiomhole. Soyinka's impatience with the complacent uncritical mass explains perhaps his excessive individualism, making him a modern hero with Napoleonic image. If UNDP factors literacy excellence as an issue in quality of life index, Soyinka's Nobel Prize undoubtedly would have improved the rating of Nigera to the position of the G-8.

For the poet and playwright, societal decay and mis-governance are no excuses for making the point that Africans are as equal and capable. Even then he never hesitates to say loudly that the war lords suffocating the continent through corruption, murder from Idi Amin to you-them-all, are as culpable. It is to the eternal credit of the poet that he refuses the temptations of being Most Senior Special Adviser (MSSA) rationalizing falsehood in the fashion of the present day motley of courtesans in the corridors of power. Soyinka passes where many Brother and Sister Jeroes surrender like the 'strongmen' of Baghdad.

Lastly, Soyinka methods are proudly and commendably civil; scholarship, wisdom, courage, commitment, patriotism through printed and spoken words and printed and written words alone. He follows in the traditions of founding fathers of Africa, namely Muhammad Ibn Abdullahi Battuta, Sultan Mansa Musa, Uthman Danfodio, Kwame Nkrumah, Nnamdi Azikiwe, Sar'dauna, Awolowo, Nelson Mandela. These are proud African civilians in their own rights who through scholarship, conviction, and perseverance, elevated Africa from subservience, servitude, ignorance, backwardness to independence, enlightenment and integrity. Soyinka shows that spoken and written words may not be as lethal as military bombs and sundry instruments of mass/individual destructions, but they are nevertheless more effective for nation building. Above all, printed and spoken words are enduring legacy for generations unborn.

Soyinka's works are undoubtedly difficult to phantom. Yours truly read WS under compulsion in school. But that's precisely the strength of the poet: obscure literacy works and collections (like Shakespeare) as distinct from easy phonograph and cheap violence, keep us (and generation unborn) positively busy to interpret and appreciate. The economics of it may even be more rewarding; student's preoccupation with Soyinka's 'Telephone Conversation' may save extra naira being expended on recharged cards on those hourly unproductive Telephone conversations that fuel capital flight by telephone operators, creates insignificant, indecent and unsustainable jobs. Long Live Soyinka!

Understanding Achebe

If there was no Achebe, a prototype would have been invented. Cynics (numerous to list) do not hesitate to enlist Achebe's as another evidence of failing governance. And they are as reductionist as to see Achebe in the light of apt classic tittles as *Things Fall Apart and No Longer at Ease.* Conversely government spokesman, Fani Kayode (a conspicuous metaphor for reaction) ever ready to do *operation fire for fire* with critics found Achebe handy to exhibit same trade marks of governmental arrogance and ignorance on subject matter that tasks knowledge and imagination. Either way we have been served by and large with heat without light, quantity as distinct from quality discourse on Achebe question. Which ever way we look at it the nation loses another opportunity for deep reflection.

This government not long ago failed Wole Soyinka's acid test when the Nobel Prize winner tasked our imagination about the deplorable state of the nation in the wake of the slain of the former Anthony General of the Federation, Chief Bola Ige. Same administration conclusively confirmed rtd. Major Umar's fears of official incompetence, insensitivity and indifference when the latter dared to speak in the face of observed national decay. Much earlier the administration had fallen cheap to the provocations of Professor Sam Aluko on the economy and Chief Ojukwu on the polity. May we for once pass Chinua Achebe's latest acid test which is far testier than the previous ones. This prayer is as valid for the government's overzealous palace jesters as it is valid for the increasing lot that has made government bashing a routine. We are all losers if the nation unwittingly confirms the Achebe's worse fear of a failed country.

Chief Presidential spokeswoman, Remi Oyo had raised the prospects of less belligerent governance when in a dignified manner she fanned ignorance about Achebe's rejection of a national award.

This unusual *water for fire* response had since been eclipsed by Fani Kayode's ever carpet bombing wrapped with star-words and demagoguery.

Fani Kayode is reactionary not so much for his ever backward parochial views but because in fairness to him he often hits the headlines in reaction to or against genuine concern about progress or lack of it. He will be remembered as the adviser on Public Affairs who never sets any public agenda but reacts against agenda setting by worthy citizens. Fani has never been counted on the side of commendation of the concerned citizens but condemnation of imaginary enemies.

We must assist government to understand Achebe with the hope that we all shall be understood. It is unhelpful that Achebe's 5 rejection paragraphs thought-for-food/food-for-thought are belittled by uncountable wounding words of Femi Fani-Kayode. Reaction to Achebe more than anything justifies why the literary giant was right to have treated the award as Greek gift as distinct from a truly national award. The government's singular intolerant reaction shows that its award was not due to added value of the recipients to the nation but government's assigned estimation of select and connected individuals that is dependent on some dubious *'political correctness'* expressed in form of sycophancy. If this government genuinely thinks Achebe deserves the award, his seemingly rude reminder of the national (*not* personal) problems makes even a greater case for same government to persuade and convince him to kindly come forward for his deserved merit. The exhibited disdain against Achebe's shows that this Presidency has a lot of job to do convincing people that it is not under the spell of men and women of little faith in what they themselves proclaim from the rooftops. It is a great paradox of this government that its yesterday's national award listed recipient turns into today's instant enemy.

The content analysis of Fani kayode's shows how this government instantly misunderstood Achebe and invariably how it is increasingly misunderstanding the nation. Achebe in this singular development will prefer reference to his book, *The Trouble with Nigeria,* which constructively deals with leadership problem. Interestingly he shares a lot in common with President Obasanjo who also in recognition of Nigeria's leadership crisis initiated and founded Leadership Forum. Achebe's reservation is all about leadership. Official reaction so far shows that leadership crisis is even deepening. It is uncharitable for anybody to remind a tested patriot like Achebe about the imperatives of national award as distinct from '*foreign and international awards in places like Sweden*' as Fani mischievously did. Achebe does not need a Nobel Prize to be noble in pursuing national agenda. That counseling from Fani is more useful for the likes of Finance Minister Ngozi Okonjo-Iweala who proudly recently celebrates receiving Europe (*not* Africa) Heroes Awards. In fact the entire administration that is desperately eager to get IMF/World bank award for 'economic recovery' even when its citizens think otherwise will find Fani's advice more homely than Achebe who as far back as independence year of 1960 proudly received the first Nigerian (not European) National Trophy for Literature.

Yasser Arafat; a Day After

According to a Nigerian saying, we are encouraged to feign death and imagine who our real foes and genuine friends are. The only exception to this singular received wisdom is that Arafat's death on Thursday 11th of November in a Paris Hospital was not a mock exercise but as real as it would be anybody's turn. But true to the old saying, a day after his death the friends and foes of Palestinians whose cause Arafat died for more than ever before became crystal clear. By their reactions and non-reactions to Arafat's death you shall know the enemies and friends of Palestinian cause.

The point cannot be overemphasised that even before he died, peer beneath the global headline-news; it was discernable who almost with applause and curious delight proclaimed Arafat '*clinically*' dead (as if death was as divisible as it was desirable). Interestingly too we know the global multitude who genuinely grieved at the sight of a sick freedom fighter (holed up for two years long in his home at Ramallah) desperately being flown for medical attention in France. It was however a day after Arafat's death with the attendant outpouring of mourns and murmurs, as they were, that Palestininans would come to terms with their friends and foes alike.

The smear campaign by the enemies before his death was that Arafat was an obstacle to peace process. Indeed the murmurs, (as distinct from genuine mourns) from Washington-London-Tel Aviv axis following his death confirmed this singular stereotype. According to Washington Arafat's exit was 'significant' suggesting that his tenure and his struggle according to Bush had been 'insignificant' in the first instance. Israeli Prime Minister Aaron Sharon minced no words saying Arafat's death was a 'turning point' and indeed an end of an era that was suggestively undesirable. Australia Prime Minister

John Howard upturned the myth about not talking bad about the dead when he reportedly remarked that '*history will judge him very harshly*' for allegedly rejecting the Israelis 2000 peace offer under Prime minister Ehud Barak. We are yet to be availed the reaction of Saddam Hussein the Iraqi dictator who Arafat in an ill-informed adventure uncritically supported during the former's aggressive campaign against Kuwait.

Assuming all these posthumous murmurs against Arafat were as valid (to the extent that his death was a turning point) a day after Arafat's death what then stops the implementation of the celebrated road map to peace and what then is the remaining obstacle to liberation of the Palestininans? Put in another way, going by the propaganda that Arafat was the problem, one expected instant Palestinian liberation rhetoric by the same anti-Arafat forces once he was buried. So far we have seen that Arafat's burial had not led to the termination of Palestinian woes.

The recently concluded Bush-Blair summit in Washington confirms the old observation that while one notorious finger was conveniently directed at Arafat (and Arafat alone), the other more culpable four fingers pointed at Washington, London (almost in that order) as the real obstacle to peace in the Middle East. International observers wondered aloud that a timely summit of two power-players, namely U.S and UK during the weekend Arafat was being buried seemed not to offer fundamental new thinking on Palestinian-Israelis war of attrition. On the contrary, in place of the old blame-Arafat game, the world is still being entertained to another new academic, non- problem solving proposals of an elongated calendar of freedom by both Blair and Bush. Time will tell who awaits the 'harsh' judgment of history; Arafat, who Nelson Mandela (him self an acknowledged freedom fighter) singled out as courageous global fighter for freedom or those from the vintage rooftops of 'civilized world' who feel ever shy to urge Israel to halt the occupation and civilian carnage in Gaza but remain ever willing to tilt foreign policy in favour of Israel.

Talking about murmurs, UN observed that Arafat's legacy was that of a leader who struggled to preserve the identity of Palestinians from extinction. Good tribute. But what happened to all UN resolutions on the occupation, Sabra and Shattila refugee massacre and two-independent states? What happens to the world court ruling on the illegality of the New Berlin wall in West bank?

Lastly about mourns. Observers scrutinise the list of African mourners at Cairo memorial and observed the conspicuous absence of President Obasanjo, chair of Africa Union. They noted that if Mr. President physically paid last tribute to the late President Ronald Reagan with all the latter's inhuman support for Apartheid South Africa, it was untenable that he sent what they perceive as a stale postal (or is it e-mail?) tribute on Arafat, a long-term friend of Africa at a time it was not fashionable to identify with the Dark Continent.

Sam Nujoma: a statesman is born

Namibia: A Nation Is Born (1981; Zed) was once a compulsory reading for all students of anti-colonialism and anti-imperialism in early 1980s. Namibia and South Africa were the last outposts of tyranny, brutal colonial occupation and Apartheid minority rule in Africa. How memory fades so soon in Africa. America together with its notable ally, Britain today claim to champion some sort of struggle against so-called "outposts" of tyranny which US Secretary of State Condoleezza Rice selectively and cynically labelled Cuba, North Korea, Iran and Zimbabwe. Interestingly history judges harshly US and its allies as oppressors in Africa. America, Britain, Germany and colonial South Africa (in that oppressive order of precedence) were the notorious, enthusiastic and ardent backers of colonial tyranny and worse forms of oppression in Namibia and South Africa as late as early 1980s. Conversely the likes of Cuba, North Korea and Islamic Republic of Iran supported the liberation movement in Namibia.

The above-referred publication was a historic work of the Information and Publicity department of South West Africa People's Organization of Namibia (SWAPO). The book was to mark the 20th anniversary of SWAPO, the national liberation movement dedicated to the total overthrow of the South Africa rule in Namibia. It prophetically predicted the liberation of Namibia. Its title was as enthusiastic as it was optimistic; *A Nation Is Born.*

True to the book's cover, Namibia was born in 1990. Thanks to the resistance of the Namibians, particularly the Hereros ably led by the likes of great African patriot, Samuel Maharero, against German land robbery in 1904. In response, the Germans perpetrated an acknowledged bare-faced genocide in history. The notorious German General Lieutenant Von Trotha issued the infamous '*Extermination*

Order' in history, "that the Herero must be destroyed as a nation", in the process, "poisoning waterholes and machine-gunning" every Herero. Indeed Hitler's later day holocaust had its root in General Trotha's experimentation in Namibia. If only the world had held the perpetrators of Namibian atrocities accountable perhaps the petty tyrants like Hitler would not have unleashed similar terrorism on a global scale in the 1940s. Paradoxically, civilized Germany still resists payment of repatriations for 1904 genocide, the greatest evidence of which was the infamous Trotha's Extermination order. Yet, the genocide only watered the seed of resistance. Germans were not only defeated but Namibians inflicted sustained assaults against the inheritor South African Apartheid colonizers.

Sam Shafishuna Nujoma, the recently retired Namibia's President and father of the Nation emerged from this great tradition of African resistance against domination and oppression. He was together with other compatriots the founding member of SWAPO, which eventually led Namibia to Independence after sustained campaign of direct actions and diplomacy. With his legendary trademarks of beards and spectacle, Nujoma is a living symbol of defiance, conviction, perseverance, independence and commitment. He was ranked 29th out of 100 greatest Africans that included legends like Mandela, Nyerere, Nkrumah and Martin Luther King by the prestigious *New African* journal.

It was a scandal that the world media maintained a low coverage of the exit of President Nujoma last moth. Woe onto African media for confirming once again that what CNN and BBC do not post on the web-sites, that is, what is not downloadable is not news worthy. It is a combination of laziness, incompetence and share irresponsibility to reduce Nujoma's retirement to a news agency two-paragraph dispatch. While Mugabe who '*had ruled Zimbabwe for the past 25 years*' hit the headline in the negativity as favoured by the Big Brother Western Media, there was a muted indifference to the historic constitutional exists of Sam Nujoma. Are we saying good-news like Sam Nujoma is too good to be African?

Sam Nujoma's Namibia has once again confirmed Walter Rodney's historic insight that colonial legacy was an abysmal disaster. Two-century colonial occupation left in its ruins pillage, destitution, illiteracy, and poverty, conversely 15 years of Independence put Namibia on medium income ranking of UNDP with education and health indicators that are above African average. Sam Nujoma was asked about his regret, his answer was developmentalist; more classrooms needed to be built for Namibian children. While Nigerian elite outdo each other in public assets stripping as witnessed in recent housing sharing scandal and budget-for-bribe scam, Nujoma's tenure showed that ruling elite could find a more rewarding preoccupation in simple but far reaching endeavour like building of schools for future generation.

Perhaps the enduring legacy of Nujoma is continuity. While Mugabe callously mowed down all compatriots like Joshua Nkomo, Nujoma showed that comradeship is as important in anti-colonial resistance as in post-colonial nation building. The ascendancy of President Hifikepunye Pohmaba as the new President of Namibia underscores the fact that Africa is not short of leaders if incumbents know that it is a long process that will outlive us all. Statesman Sam Nujoma is welcome to the Hall of Fame of great Africans who know when to allow other compatriots advance the struggle for development just as Nyerere, Kaunda and Mandela competently set the pace not because the West favoured it but because Africans are better off without sit-tight messiahs.

Return of Walter Rodney

Dr Tajudeen Abdulraheem in his weekly 'Around the World'* commendably brought home the June 13th activities marking the 25th anniversary of the callous murder of Walter Rodney in his home country, Guyana. He urged readers to visit the website of the Walter Rodney International Commemoration Committee for fuller reports and similar solidarity manifestations around the world. Yours truly went to the site and discovered that activity marking the anniversary of Rodney's death in Africa was as token as it was insignificant, if not completely unremarkable. In contrast to the seemingly disinterested great chroniclers like Basil Davidson and Thomas Pakenham, Walter Rodney (very well in the traditions of Frantz Fanon, Bala Usman, Mahmud Tukur) had written the history of Africa with intense passion and unapologetic ownership of a process they themselves helped to deepen through their own acknowledged radical engagement.

An African-Guyanese, Rodney's works were both in quantity and quality on Africa. His PhD thesis at the record age of 24 was on '*History of the Upper Guinea Coast, 1545-1800*). Walter was (and is) more known with the classic work; *How Europe Underdeveloped Africa* which at publication in 1972, reviewers likened to

> '...a mighty, uplifting gust of fresh air' without romanticising pre-colonial Africa 'had placed it in the context of human development across the globe, traced its real historical relationships to the colonizing forces of Europe and suggested path for Africa's movement toward a new life for its people and a new role in the re-shaping of the world.'

---

* *Weekly Trust* 25/7/2005

Walter's had similar impact on African consciousness just as Frantz Fanon's *Wretched of the Earth* had on liberation and freedom consciousness globally in the 1960s.

The most unsavoury commentary about Rodney remembrance is Nigeria where no known manifestation is in place either within or outside the universities or civil society to acknowledge the contributions of this great African scholar. For a country whose leaders, media columnists (fifth?) and writers alike recently were in competition for space to celebrate the life and times of late America's President Ronald Regan, Walter Rodney undoubtedly from the grave observed with keen interest *How Africans Underdeveloped Africa through Memory Loss and Misplaced Recollections/Priorities.*

The challenge of Rodney's remembrance lies in reinventing Walter Rodney not in a Jesuit way (he was not a Prophet) but in a creative way to reinvent history and historic methodology in our development process. It is a sad commentary that Africans forget so soon where we were coming from, thus get quickly frustrated with the present and consequently proved incapable of discerning what the future will be. The missing link is nothing but loss of memory and retrenchment of history in our daily life. The official sermon about patriotism and African renaissance comes to nothing unless we come to terms with history and historical approach. Those who ignore the past repeat it in a most dastardly way. Libya's Gaddafi needed not remind African leaders about the futility of begging for aids and credits if AU chieftains have the knowledge of history to appreciate the fact that a century of European colonialism did not build a factory nor train a doctor.

Sadly in the age of market forces, school graduates are seen as hunters and gatherers of jobs (not citizens) in the labour market, for jobs that are increasingly never there. In the process, we have relegated history to the background in the curriculum under the banner of the so-called functional education whose functionality is only measurable in relations to 419, individualism, low productivity, cronyism, betrayal, certified illiteracy, looting of common wealth and complete servitude to anything branded foreign. Ask a university 'graduate' desperate to enlist for 'lottery visa' about slavery, colonialism and struggle for Independence and appreciate the 'functionality' of our 'functional education'.

In reinventing Walter Rodney, we must urgently come to terms with the issue of development. His concern is about development and underdevelopment of Africa and nothing more. His holistic useful approach to the naughty issue of development contrasts sharply with the unhelpful frustrating 'economistic' on-the-one-hand-approach of many African leaders today. Some 45 years after Independence, we are even "Development"-shy as IMF/World Bank push 'ownership' of adjustment and reform/poverty alleviation programmes *not* development/wealth generation programmes. Paradoxically, we are measured every year by Development Index, long identified by Rodney and *not* reform index.

Lastly the return of Walter Rodney means we must critically revisit Rodney's assumptions of the 1960s and 1970s and avoid the pitfalls of romanticization of Rodney himself. To what extent can we be hunted by colonialism and slavery? It is not Europeans who looted the treasury in the shameful traditions of Mobutu and made looted funds a factor of national budget as in the case of Nigeria. It is not Europeans who mowed down all opposition figures like Ndabaningi Sithole, Abel Muzorewa and Joshua Nkomo as Mugabe is doing in Zimbabwe. It is African leaders (or are they dealers) like Uganda's Yoweri Muzeveni who organizes a phoney and predictable wasteful patronizing referendum to ask Ugandans who were born into multipartism, whether they deserve what is plainly their legitimate democratic heritage 45 years after. Walter Rodney might be right to observe that the balance sheet of colonialism carried no 'credits'. But colonialist Lugard's Nigeria built railway line from Lagos in 1896 to Kano in 1911, a total of 711 miles within 15 years certainly to foster the goal of exploitation but 45 years after we have left this standard gauge to rust even as billions meant to revamp Railways have gone to you-know-them all. Colonialism, Rodney wrote had only one hand-'It was a one armed bandit'. What would he have said of independent Africa under many African leaders today?

Who Speaks For Nigeria After Bala Usman?

So long a week. It was weighty enough to come to terms with the sudden death of the Executive Director of Civil Liberty Organization (CLO) and my comrade, Chima Ubani, on the 21st of September. It was certainly one death too many to then face up to another reality of the death of the great chronicler and my teacher, Dr Yusuf Bala Usman. And as I was putting finishing touch to this reflection news came of the death of Mr. Aka Bashorun, one-time President of Nigeria Bar Association (NBA), a progressive patriotic advocate of Nigeria, a worthy mentor. As vulnerable consummate mortals we pretend to sympathies with the dead when in reality the burden is on the living that must carry on where the dead stopped. In fact it is we the living who need sympathy given the enormous tasks of unfinished agenda for here and hereafter.

With specific reference to Dr Yusuf Bala's exit who more than added his own value, the burden is Nigeria's which has suddenly lost a singular voice of defence at a time of sustained attack from sundry enemies that include revisionist "historians", Senior Advocates of Nigeria, paid government officials and their unapologetic and even celebrated anti-Nigerian policies.

The exhibited national sense of loss which trails Usman's death confirms the observation that it is the country that is pained. As significant as the outpouring of acknowledgement of his works is, labeling Usman "radical" and a "social critic" only name him but do not in any way help in appreciating the significance of his singular contribution to national development. In fact social labeling is what Bala would have dismissed as a "misrepresentation" of his pan African engagement that tasked body and brain so long. Naming Bala does not tame the volumes of printed words about the way forward for Nigeria.

Very few scholars of Bala's intellectual resources have generously deployed such scarce intellectual resources at the service of the nation as Bala did in the past four decades. Many have left and relocated but Bala lived and died in Zaria making a case for Nigeria and Africa. Very few have such staying and enduring power.

The article "Three myths about the Formation of Nigeria" in the book, *The Misrepresentation of Nigeria*, co-authored with Akasumu Abba is a compulsory reading for those willing to appreciate the depth of Bala's generous advocacy for Nigeria. The book was written in 2000. There has been some resurgence of self doubt about nation-building project and indiscriminate dubious claims on the country's history and geography. The referred article more than anything else, restored faith of many Nigerians in Nigerian project.

The first myth was that Nigeria's history started with the amalgamation in 1914 by Lord Lugard. 1914 had become the reference point for those who suddenly found it fashionable to question the viability of Nigerian state and doubt the process of national integration. Paradoxically those who promote this distortion of history include those who without "amalgamation" would not have been known for what they are today. I recall that one notable distortionist was Chief Richard Akinjide, a *Senior Advocate of Nigeria* and former Attorney General of the Federation. According to him, Nigeria "cannot work" because of the "mistake of 1914" through which the British "wanted the poor man of the North to marry the wealthy lady of the South." Bala shows with indisputable data that contrary to the received wisdom, 1914 itself is a product of serial amalgamations of diverse Nigerian communities (not geographical laagers called North and South) dating back to 1893 with respect to Niger Coast Protectorate, 1906 with respect to colony of Lagos and 1900 with respect to the protectorate of Northern Nigeria (made up of autonomous emirates like Sokoto caliphates, kingdom of Borno, Jukun and Igala kingdoms among others).

The import of this historic insight is that the new Doubting Thomases of our time have a lot to interrogate and doubt beyond Nigeria of 1914. Let them look at other "mistakes" such as the "mistakes" of colony of Lagos, of Northern Protectorate, Niger Coast protectorate. It is debatable if the country's National Orientation Agency with all its resources can boast of this singular spirited intellectual defence of Nigeria project as Bala generously did.

The second myth deals with the simplistic categories bandied around to describe the complex reality of Nigeria; namely "North", "South", "Hausa-Fulani", "Igbo", "Yoruba", "Muslims" and "Christians" and upon which we formulate policies. Bala courageously problematised these social labels which we falsely see as "fixed" and "immutable" and concluded that they "...obscure the mosaic plurality of Nigeria and Nigerians and the processes of fusions, diffusions, intermeshing, formations and transformations, which have marked the history of the peoples of the Nigerian area for millennia."

The last significant contribution of the great historian was exposing the myth of Nigeria's arbitrary creation. Agreeing with the findings of notable historians like Emeritus Professor Ade Ajayi and Professor Alagua, Dr Bala reminded us of the natural "geographical compactness" of Nigeria which made not only colonial amalgamations imperative but which explains the age long interactions between the diverse peoples of Nigeria.

The question is; after Bala who dares to take up the challenge of advocacy for Nigeria and expose more myths being manufactured every day to deny development, national integration and repositioning of Nigeria in the comity of nations? The greatest tribute to Dr Yusuf Bala is to factor history and memory to the country's development process from schools to offices, from corporate board rooms to government houses. The possibility is that strong memory will insulate the country against the hurricane of increasing local and global centrifugal forces. This however calls for a new official mindset that does not pitch one knowledge against the other, appreciates the value of knowledge in general and history in particular. So long a week before the 45th Independence anniversary in which patriots have suddenly become endangered species.

Alao-Aka Bashorun - lessons in *patriotism*

This weekend in Lagos, the remains of the former President of Nigeria Bar Association (NBA), late Alao Aka Bashorun will be laid to eternal rest. If there should be a worthy epitaph that captures many national value additions of the legendary activist lawyer it should read: A *Patriot to the core.* Patriotism is certainly out of fashion nowadays. No thanks to the elitist slide back to regionalism, parochialism, narrow-mindedness, shameless chauvinism and new slavery as political leadership uncritically joins the bandwagon of globalization via cancerous neo-liberalism unapologetically practiced in the breach by its very proponents. It is therefore understandable that only few endangered species called *patriots* will appreciate the significance of Aka's patriotism and how Nigeria has once again lost a voice after the death of the likes of Dr Bala Usman and Chima Ubani. Yet until the latest leap into reaction and backwardness, it was a mark of singular honour and progress to be so privileged as a patriot in the mould of nationalists; Jaja of Opobo, Ajayi Bishop Crowther, Raji Abdallah, Michael Imoudu, Sa'ad Zungur, Aminu Kano, Nnamdi Azikiwe, Ahmadu Bello, Obafemi Awolowo, etc. In fact the inspiration for this tribute was drawn from one of the numerous history tittles of Emeritus Professor Ade Ajayi dedicated to *A Patriot To The Core: Bishop Ajayi Crowther.*

Aka was an unofficial Senior Advocate of Nigeria dating back to colonial era. Paradoxically he was not so honoured with official SAN by the law bureaucracy before his death. In fact, the great irony is that those so generously privileged as official advocates of Nigeria are now in the habit of questioning the existence of Nigeria altogether. For instance Chief Richard Akinjide (SAN), one-time Anthony General of the Federation in a scandalous historic revisionism suddenly realised that amalgamation of "1914 was a mistake", an opportunistic fallacy contrary to the recorded facts by great chroniclers like Ade Ajayi, E.J. Alagoa and Bala Usman. It was to the eternal credit of late Aka Bashorun that despite being denied official appointments and not parasitically drawing on the state through appointments but officially harassed for exposing the limitations of mediocre governance, he kept abiding faith in Nigeria and Nigerians until his incapacitation six years ago and eventual death last month. While the likes of Dr Frederick Fashehun of the notorious OPC buckled under the weight of military dictatorship, betrayed patriotic faith and slide back from socialism and democracy to tribalism; Aka Bashorun raised the banner of democracy, nationhood, pan-Africanism and internationalism to the end.

He was on the barricade together with other patriotic first generation Nigerian students in the 1960s denouncing Anglo-Nigeria defence pact in the knowledge that the promise of independence was not neo-colonialism. His remarkable reinvention of the hitherto moribund Bar, as the President of NBA, during the dark days of military dictatorship only increased the noise level of his strident advocacy for Nigeria. Prior to NBA leadership challenge his comrades including yours sincerely knew as much that he *worshiped* and *worked* for Nigeria. Aka Bashorun Law Chambers at Jebba West in Lagos was the Nigeria's equivalent of legendary Mandela-Oliver legal office at Fox Street Johannesburg which opened doors to justice and fairness for the multitude of the oppressed and under privileged. Jebba West was a market-place of ideas and activities for freedom, anti-Apartheid, democracy and socialism, perceived then as "subversion" by the status quo. Aka Bashorun was a meticulous lawyer who shared traditions with famous progressive lawyers who put law at the service of the oppressed such as South Africa's late Yusuf Dadoo, Alfred Nzo, Nelson Mandela and Oliver Tambo.

Reading General Babangida making a case for the recently concluded national confab without acknowledging the fact the likes of Aka Bashorun and others were once persecuted by his regime for such advocacy shows that time is longer rope. Aka Chambers was also a remarkable platform for national integration. Not few lawyers have passed through the chambers that included Bob Manuel, Femi Falana, Tony Akika, among others.

In particular and of special significance is the fact that Aka Bashorun will be remembered for his comradeship and generosity. Socialism was not for him a slogan of convenience or passing fad to seek relevance and prominence but a means for practical deeds to lift those lagging behind in the rat race of life under capitalism. Yours truly, late Dr Bala Muhammed and Chom Bagu Deme were direct beneficiaries of his generosity and solidarity. He single-handedly handed our case against Ango-Abdulalhi inspired repressive mass expulsion of 1981 in ABU Zaria. My indebtedness even borders on romanticism precisely because I own my first air travel to him in the 1980s. A remarkable elegant and successive advocate, Aka Bashorun was conscious of the limitations of law as tool for transformation. He told us that we could only get judgement and not necessarily justice in the court during our battle against expulsion. He accordingly advised that we return back to school even if it entailed starting afresh adding that nothing was too much (including time) in search for knowledge. We own heap of certificates today to Aka Bashorun's worthy counseling. One cannot be too grateful to a worthy patriot. Aka's *well having* and *well giving* was never done in the full glare of TV camera or pages of newspapers given his exceptional modesty. I am certainly confident that was he alive today, Aka would have been embarrassed by the enthusiasm of our gratitude as beneficiaries of his solidarity. May Almighty Allah grant him eternal rest.

Mugabe at 80

"The Greater the Visible Order, the Greater the Hidden Disorder"
- Ben Okri, *A Way of Being Free*

President Robert Mugabe of Zimbabwe recently marked his 80th birthday. According to him, he is still very much active in politics, even as he signifies willingness (sic) to retire in 2008. Mugabe, the man, Zimbabwean opposition media derides as '*Big-Mouth*' reportedly boasts to say that he still remains the key actor in Zimbabwe's political terrain for quite a long time to come. Discussing Mugabe puts objectivity on trial. No Head of State has further polarised a distressed continent in recent times as Mugabe. The road Libya's Gadafi increasingly finds thorny is where Mugabe finds smooth. It is either you are '*for*' or '*against*' *a 'liberation fighter', 'a land grabber', 'a dictator'*, ad infinitum. Yet, as controversial as Mugabe will ever be, we must still come to terms with an African statesman at 80.

Mugabe's life (political life) seems inversely related with Zimbabwean progress. One time Maoist guerrilla fighter, famous for his African print wear at pre-independence Lancaster Summit, a man imprisoned for well over a decade, but emerged as post-colonial leader in 1980 now 24 years with three-piece suit (no more African print) has truly come of age. Mugabe has undoubtedly survived and put his imprint on the Zimbabwean map. But how has Zimbabwe fared under his two-decade rule? Zimbabwean dollar was 8 to 1 in 1995, today, it is 6000 to 1. Price riot is the norm with the inflation at 600 percent. Unemployment is 70 per cent. The political class is far more bitterly divided than at independence. 'Treasonable trials' arrests, draconian laws, detention and persecution of opponents, characteristics of colonial settlers' rule are now common features of

Mugabe's Zimbabwe. We may engage in academic sophistry identifying reasons for the forces responsible for today's Zimbabwean decay no less than we may explain why colonial settlers, subdued the African people in the 1890s. Yours truly is not unaware of some of these 'reasons'. One reason is the alleged conspiracy of the gang of three, namely British's Tony Blair, Jack Straw and the American's George Bush to strangulate Zimbabwe following the land reform that disposed few white settlers and returned land back to the disposed blacks. We are reminded of the 'smart' sanctions, which include the suspension from Zimbabwe of the Common Wealth and denial of Zimbabwe's access to IMF/World Bank aid and credit on the prodding of Britain and USA. Another reason is the 'subversive' and 'disruptive' politics of opposition represented by Tsavangirai's MDC. As alluring as these reasons are, they only explain but do not in anyway invalidate the truism that despair statistics is fastly regaining hope in the last ten years of Mugabe's long rule. The truth of the matter is that Mugabe is fatigued. He has run out of creative ideas to move Zimbabwe forward and must necessarily bow out now before Zimbabwe collapses under the weight and the rot of his dictatorial unaccountable rule. It is a sad commentary that a land blessed with notable leaders like Joshua Nkomo, Ndabaningi Sithole, James Chikerema, Josiah Tongogara, Herbert Chitepo, Abel Muzerewa as at independence is today begging for notable successors, no thanks to Mugabe's long-dated repression of opposition. It is a sad footnote on Mugabe's rule that colonialism threw up more qualititative leaders than Mugabe's rule tolerated. Twenty years after, opposition is as mediocre as his dictatorship.

Mugabe's celebrated land reform is belated and diversionary. It was actually Nkomo's ZAPU which first championed land reform by frontally questioning the 1979 Lancaster agreement's ambiguous principle of willing sellers/buyers. Mugabe ZANU's answer was war of attrition in Matabele land, ZAPU's political strong hold with unforgetfully brutality of the notorious 5th brigade. Mugabe is one 'liberator' who deployed instruments meant for his enemies against the opposition, made up of his own people. Almost like Sadam Hussein. With all the reported current forceful land seizures, the alleged violence against the white settlers is still nothing compared to the criminal violence in Metebeland in the wake of Independence in 1980, apparently without opposition (certainly with the support) from UK and America. The latest Mugabe's new mask of a '*Commonwealth conqueror*' (sounds like Idi Amin) is also deceptive. Since when? The Harare declaration (Mugabe's acid-test) was made in Zimbabwe and not in London with his then enthusiastic support. In 1991, he hosted the Commonwealth dining with the Queen and playing rugby with Australian Prime Minister, Bob Hawke. When Nigeria was suspended from the Commonwealth on account of bad governance in 1995, Mugabe never staged a walk-out in solidarity with Nigeria. But today he expects same solidarity instead of enthroning good governance. There may be conspiracy against Zimbabwe, but conspiracy only germinates on a fertile soil, the type under the heel of Mugabe. The point cannot be overemphasised that the responsibility for food shortages, inflation, and human and trade union rights' violations as well as abysmal performance of Zimbabwe team during the Tunisia 2004 soccer campaign, in the final analysis, is Mugabe's at 80 and *not* with Britain Blair's, Jack Straw or America's Bush or Queen's Commonwealth. By the way, kindly compare Mugabe's 80th birthday with Mandela's 80th birthday and spot the difference between exclusion and narrow mindedness and inclusiveness and broadmindedness, between reaction and progress respectively.

Reinventing Walter Rodney

June 13th, this year, marked the 25th anniversary of the tragic death of Dr Walter Rodney in his home country Guyana. In contrast with the seemingly disinterested great chroniclers like Basil Davidson and Thomas Pakenham, Walter Rodney (very well in the traditions of Frantz Fanon, Bala Usman, Mahmud Tukur) had written the history of Africa with intense passion and unapologetic ownership of a process he himself helped to deepen through his acknowledged radical mix of theory and practice.

An African-Guyanese, Rodney's works were both in quantity and quality on Africa. His PhD thesis at the record age of 24 was on '*History of the Upper Guinea Coast, 1545-1800*). Walter was (and still is) more known with the classic work; *How Europe Underdeveloped Africa* which at publication in 1972, reviewers likened to '…a mighty, uplifting gust of fresh air'. Without romanticising pre-colonial Africa he placed the continent 'in the context of human development across the globe, traced its real historical relationships to the colonizing forces of Europe and suggested path for Africa's movement toward a new life for its people and a new role in the re-shaping of the world.' Walter's had similar impact on African consciousness just as *Frantz Fanon's Wretched of the Earth* had on liberation and freedom consciousness globally in the 1960s.

It is sad a commentary that no known manifestation took place in Nigeria either within or outside the universities or civil society to acknowledge the contributions of this great African scholar, whose works drew heavily from the bagful of the past struggles, enterprise and industry of Nigerian peoples. Not long ago, Nigerian leaders, media columnists and writers alike were in competition for space to celebrate the life and times of late America's President Ronald Regan, whose visitation to the Dark Continent was through bombing of Tripoli. Walter Rodney undoubtedly from the grave observes with keen interest *How Africans Underdeveloped Africa through Memory Loss and Misplaced Recollections / Commentaries.*

The challenge of remembrance lies in reinventing Walter Rodney not in a Jesuit way (he was not a Prophet) but in a creative way to reinvent history and historic methodology in our development process and above all in our schools. Africans forget so soon where we were coming from, thus get quickly frustrated with the present and consequently proved incapable of discerning what the future will be. The missing link is nothing but loss of memory and retrenchment of history in our daily life. The official sermon about patriotism and African renaissance comes to nothing unless we come to terms with history and historical approach. Those who ignore the past repeat it in a most dastardly way. They are even rudely talked at. Libya's Gaddafi needed not remind African leaders about the futility of begging for aids and credits if AU chieftains have the knowledge of history to appreciate the fact that a century of European colonialism did not build a factory nor train a doctor.

Sadly in the age of market forces, school graduates are seen as hunters and gatherers of jobs in the labour market not citizens worthy of mastering the past. Consequently, we have relegated history to the background in the curriculum. The former governor of Osun State, Chief Bisi Akande in one breath criminalized history subjects, sacked humanity teachers even as he denied 'science' tutors monthly pay. The result is the so-called functional education, whose functionality is only measurable in relations to 419, individualism, low productivity, cronyism, betrayal, certified illiteracy, looting of common wealth and complete servitude to anything branded foreign. Ask a university 'graduate' desperate to enlist for 'lottery visa' about slavery, colonialism and struggle for Independence and appreciate the 'functionality' of our 'functional education'.

In reinventing Walter Rodney, we must urgently come to terms with the issue of development. His concern is about development and underdevelopment of Africa and nothing more. His holistic useful approach to the naughty issue of development contrasts sharply with the unhelpful frustrating on-the-one-hand-approach of many African leaders today. Some 45 years after Independence and many years after Rodney identified critical success factors in development; we are shamelessly still "Development"-shy. IMF/ World Bank and donors push 'ownership' of adjustment and reform/poverty alleviation programmes *not* development/wealth generation programmes. In any case nowhere in history was development patronizingly ascribed. Development is always achieved by those who desire it and in spite of those who strive to deny it. Paradoxically, we are measured every year by Development Index by UNDP, long identified by Rodney and *not* reform index feverishly sold by creditors.

Reinventing Walter Rodney demands that we also critically revisit Rodney's assumptions of the 1960s and 1970s and avoid the pitfalls of romanticization of Rodney himself, again in the tradition of the great scholar who teaches that the only thing constant is dialectics and change. To what extent can we be hunted permanently by the spectre of colonialism and slavery? It is not Europeans who looted the treasury in the shameful traditions of Mobutu and made looted funds a factor of national budget as in the case of Nigeria. It is not Europeans who mowed down all opposition figures like Ndabaningi Sithole, Abel Muzorewa and Joshua Nkomo as Mugabe is doing in Zimbabwe. It is African leaders who annulled elections with a thousand and one reasons. It is African leaders (or are they dealers?) like Uganda's Yoweri Muzeveni who organize a phoney and predictable wasteful patronizing referendum to ask Ugandans who were born into multipartism, whether they deserve what is unquestionably their legitimate democratic heritage 45 years after. It was Samuel Doe and Charles Taylor not Lugard who fuelled a war of attrition, cutting limps and fingers in Sierra Leone very well in the brutal tradition of Belgian campaign in the Congo. Walter Rodney might be right to observe that the balance sheet of colonialism carried no 'credits'. But colonialist Lugard's Nigeria built railway line from Lagos in 1896 to Kano in 1911, a total of 711 miles within 15 years undoubtedly to foster the goal of exploitation. Some 45 years after we have left this standard gauge to rust even as billions meant to revamp Railways have gone to you-know- them all. Colonialism, Rodney wrote had only one hand-'*It was a one armed bandit*'. What would he have said of the hydra-headed banditry of many post-colonial African leaders?

In Celebration of Life*

Consciously yours sincerely holds that my new book, *Tears Not Enough*, passes for *Reflections of Passion* in the true spirit of Yanni's collections, the American Greek master of passion on electronic key board. But I never bargained that the book's public presentation together with another entitled the *End of Industry* downtown Ilorin during the weekend as part of my 45th birth day ended in *celebration of life* again true to Yanni's keyboard calling. Many thanks to all who took time out to mark life in a country in which mourning, disasters and funerals have become a ritual, the latest being Ilado pipeline (read: poverty) disaster in which as many as 300 got consumed in fire. In 1999, as many as that figure were consumed by similar fire in Jesse. Seven years after what was thought to be a disastrous exception had since become the rule; pipe-line explosions, mass charred bodies, official belated probes, then another explosion ad infinitum.

Thanks to Almighty Allah for sparing our lives in the past four and half decades. Ultimately it is not our strength as such but that of Almighty Allah. The Quran says it all; "And if you would count the grace of Allah, never could you be able to count them" (Quran 14:34). Many thanks to the people and governments of Kwara, Kano, Kaduna and Kano for their solidarity at such short notice. It is remarkable how I have undergone such an identity transformation from a country boy in Kwara to a multinational citizen of the world.

My eternal gratitude to the chairman of the book presentation, Justice Mustapha Akanbi - a father, an unapologetic comrade in his own right who at that age copiously quoted great thinkers to make a point that Nigeria's future is bright in spite of the current despair.

* *Daily Trust*, 15th May 2006

Celebrating life also brings to the fore the virtue of family ties and friendship. I have been privileged with family love that flows from my wife, children and countless relatives. As for friends, a proverb has it that "a friend at hand is better than a far distant relative".

Friends in large number and profound quality were at hand during the weekend in Ilorin to celebrate life well beyond my imagination. The significance of the attendance is that the friends cut across our artificial cutting edges: from trade unions (my constituencies) to corporate businesses to government officials.

It was Nelson Mandela who enjoined us to "…be ready to give back to society part of what we gain from it." My two books constitute a pay back to the society that nurtured me out of nothing to something worthy of celebrating.

A Zimbabwe wisdom has it that "when there is a mountain in your path, do not sit down at its foot and cry, get up and climb it". My life so far shows that if there is the will there must be many ways. Of special importance is that as a child of independence we were privileged to grow up at interesting times. In the 1960s, leaders were performers and gentlemen. In fact the late Prime Minister was so described in his autobiography as "Honourable Gentleman". Pray how many leaders can be so described today? Precisely because the country's leaders were then honourable, we were honoured with good education, good health, good community which sustained life and enhanced life-expectancy. In 1983, Chinua Achebe wrote that: "the Nigerian problem is the unwillingness of its leaders to rise to the challenge of personal example, which is the hallmark of true leadership." Achebe wrote that when leadership was assuming a crisis proportion. Now that we are having a leadership scourge, what will Achebe write? As the debate for and against you know it all (sad, sorry third term!) rages on, hundreds at Ilado got burnt in avoidable inferno, power outages continue and factory closures continue unabated yet this serial disaster will only hit the head line for a moment before we return to business as usual.

Essential Mandela At 88*

Comrade Madiba, former President of Republic of South Africa will be 88 tomorrow. In his own words on the marble; "I was born in Umtata, Transkei, on 18th July 1918. My father died in 1930, after which David Dalindyebo, then acting Paramount Chief of the tribe, became my guardian."

Madiba is currently a grand-grand father, a pensioner, a statesman and an activist against HIV/AIDS and a powerful voice for world peace and social justice. But in celebrating Nelson Rolihlahla Mandela's birthday, the issue of leadership readily comes to the fore. It is a great paradox that a globally acknowledged leader comes from a continent that suffers from huge leadership deficit from Harare to Banjul, from Abuja to Cairo!

Mandela is a classic study in value-based leadership. Leadership has been described as a "*process of directing the behaviour of others towards the accomplishment of some common objectives*". There is a broad consensus of opinion that nobody has shaped the behaviour of humanity in the direction of steadfastness, perseverance, sacrifices, reconciliation and above all forgiveness like Nelson Mandela. Many theories of leadership abound, from the ascribed, the achieved to the latest silly sergeant-major type being shamelessly propagated for Nigeria by the likes of sergeant, sorry Senator David Mark. History will however record it that what Nelson Mandela gives the world is value-based leadership that stresses civility not barrack jack-boot, democracy not dictatorship, integrity, honesty of purpose, selflessness, disinterestedness, forgiveness and non-vengeance.

---

* Daily Trust, 17th July 2006

As Nigeria prepares for a transition from one "civilian" administration to another, all contenders for varying offices are enjoined to appreciate the qualities of Nelson Mandela if only they want to make a radical departure from the existing mediocrity, wars of attrition, unnecessary violence to issues-based contestation and cooperation and development.

One essential feature of Mandela's leadership type is knowledge. Even though of unlettered parentage, Mandela struggled from illiteracy to multiple degrees that included a bachelor degree of Arts. Indeed he is a qualified lawyer and solicitor. Not even the mental and physical torture of dark 27 years on Robben Island was a barrier to the search for knowledge. Mandela in his memoirs, "*Long Walk to Freedom*" observed that, "As freedom fighters and political prisoners, we had an obligation to improve and strengthen ourselves, and study was one of the few opportunities to do so." A critical reading of Madiba' speeches, writings and documents from 1940s to date show that these are not cold and detached words of hired speech- writers of most modern day African leaders but enduring words of an informed leader conscious of his claims and the responsibilities that go with them. Read these eternal words for instance and see how Mandela have kept faith with every word he mustered during the great Rivonia Trial on 20th April 1964 at Pretoria Supreme Court;

> "During my lifetime I have dedicated myself to this struggle of the African people. I have fought against white domination, and I have fought against black domination. I have cherished the ideal of a democratic and free society in which all persons live together in harmony and with equal opportunities. It is an ideal which I hope to live for and to achieve. But if needs be, it is an ideal for which I am prepared to die."

In celebrating Mandela today, the point cannot be overemphasised that Nigeria and indeed Africa need knowledge-driven leadership that makes conscious choice for development and willing to see it through just as Mandela made conscious choice for freedom and saw it through. He promised not to replace white domination with black, he did. He promised to uphold the banner of democracy he did such that he left when the popular uproar was for him to stay and at a time Mugabes and Musevenis are sitting tight even when they are unwanted.

The second essential feature of Nelson Mandela is forgiveness and reconciliation, traits of remarkable qualitative personality that have navigated South Africa from the brink of annihilation to unparallel rainbow nation with unprecedented multi-racial growth and development. Regardless of the political divide, world leaders are unanimous about the spirit of forgiveness of Nelson Mandela. Witness what former US President Bill Clinton has to say about him:

> "For a long time the name Nelson Mandela has stood for the quest for freedom. His spirit never bent before the injustice of his 27 years of imprisonment. Apartheid could not silence him ... After his long struggle, Nelson Mandela found in himself the strength to reach out to others; to build up instead of tear down. He led his country forward, always choosing reconciliation over division. This is the miracle of the new South Africa. Time and again, President Mandela showed real wisdom and rose above bitterness. President Mandela and the South African people, both black and white, have inspired others around the world."

And compare this to Fidel Castro of Cuba:

> "Nelson Mandela will not go down in history for the 27 consecutive years that he lived imprisoned without ever renouncing his ideas. He will go down in history because he was able to draw from his soul all the poison accumulated by such an unjust punishment. He will be remembered for his generosity and for his wisdom at the time of an already uncontainable victory, when he knew how to lead so brilliantly his self-sacrificing and heroic people, aware that the new South Africa would never be built on foundations of hatred and revenge."

It to the eternal credit of Madiba that during his tenure no previous racist opponent has been oppressed the manner he was brutally treated. On the contrary, on the day of his inauguration he paid glowing tributes to the likes of Fredrick De Klerk for their courage to accept the reality of new liberated South Africa. Will Nigerian politicians learn from the spirit of Nelson Mandela's forgiveness starting with President Olusegun Obasanjo and his deputy, Atiku Abubakar to banish their quarrel and move the nation forward? Happy birth day Madiba!

Ghana At 50: Nkrumah's Second Coming*

"Ghana was the beginning, our first liberated zone. Thirty-seven years later – in 1994 – we celebrated our final triumph when Apartheid was crushed and Nelson Mandela was installed as the president of South Africa. Africa's long struggle for freedom was over." - *Former Tanzanian President, Late Julius Nyerere, 1997*

My first trip outside Nigeria was to Ghana, the first African country that fought and won independence from British imperialism in 1957, 50 years last week. My trip was in 1982. Ghana was the last sanctuary in my search of knowledge after Ango-Abdullahi Vice-Chancellorship (read; professorial dictatorship) hounded us via the criminal resolution of Committee of Vice Chancellors according to which 1981 expelled ABU activists ought not to be admitted into any Nigerian university. In search of readmission I landed in Accra that was certainly down and out, no thanks to bad governance of incompetent and corrupt Generals (Ankrah, Afrifa, Akuffo, Acheampong-in that-other). These *politi-Generals* like most of their discredited counterparts in the sub-region were afflicted by what late Amilca Cabra aptly described as "*cancer of betrayal*" which was what pushed them to cowardly overthrow Nkrumah in February 1966, barely a month there was a similar dastardly military onslaught in Nigeria. Since 1982, yours sincerely had sojourned Lagos-Accra umpteenth times virtually by air. Every trip was hunted by my first singular experience of acute human deprivations in Ghana of the 80s. The spirit of Accra is that of amazing African recovery that beats all imagination. Ghana's total collapse was so deafening in the eighties

* Daily Trust, 12th March 2007

that I could not take the offer of an admission at Legon University because all the lecturers were in Nigeria hunting and gathering a living denied. As a matter of fact, three quarter of my lecturers in Uniport (where I ended my graduate studies) turned out to be Ghanaians. The spectacular picture of desperate Ghanaians retuning home with legendary *Ghana-Must-Go* bags (of basics like soaps, *Geisha* and *toothpaste)* contrasts today with a favoured proud people that boasts of relatively better life expectancy in a generally depressed sub region. In fact, it is now a reversed movement. Nigerians now mass-exodus to Accra either as students (Ghanaian teachers are back home!) or tourists escaping from power outages and armed robbery/terrorism of Lagos.

Last Monday, I arrived in Ghana, (deliberately by road to keep date with history, an experience that constitutes another reflection) for the 50th independence anniversary. I arrived with burst-and-boom perception of Ghana. But I dare confess that I for ever share boom-and-boom perspective of this great country, after witnessing the 50th independence anniversary celebration. My last week trip was filled with special passion and nostalgia. As a student of history and decolonization in particular, Ghana is a total commitment to memory not just a flash of the moment. As a child of independent Africa, witnessing Ghana at 50, made history remarkably simpler than my countless but great history teachers taught me. I bear witness that unlike Nigeria, Ghana kept memory alive.

There was an enactment of Ghana independence declaration at the Old Polo Ground in Accra on Monday, 5th of July. This singular historic global manifestation brought back deep feelings and excitements that characterised the declaration of Ghana's Independence on March 6th, 1957 by the founding President Osagyefo Dr. Kwame Nkrumah. Yours sincerely remains averse to simplistic personality view of history which holds that a country's historical development is explainable on account of leadership types, styles and methods. Yet the historic reality of Ghana and indeed Africa, (as distinct from our individual preference), shows that the energy, visions, ideas and methods of Nkrumah were central to the liberation of the continent from colonial rule. Not even Nelson Mandela with his larger-than-memory status obliterates the unique role of Nkrumah in the liberation of the continent. On the contrary, Mandela himself noted that the events of 1957 in Accra which led to the pulling down of the Union Jack of Imperial Britain and its replacement by Red, Gold and Green flag of a new Ghana (formerly Gold Coast) were sources of inspiration for the battle against Apartheid, the last draconian face of colonialism. This explains while with all his party (New Patriotic Party, NPP) aversion to Nkrumah's legacy, President John Kufor mentioned Nkrumah more than four times and paid special homage to the legend in his independence at the independence square on March 6th.

The anti-climax was the "second coming" of Nkrumah as it were. The ace actor, David Dontoh, acted Dr Nkrumah, surrounded by his 5 other compatriots (making the big civilian six, namely; Obetsebi Lampley, Arke Adjei, Williams Ofori Atta, Dr J. B. Danquah and Akufo-Addo.). They broke the midnight silence with the declaration of Independence at the same location Nkrumah stood at the Polo Ground (now transformed into the Nkrumah Mausoleum). Many Ghanaians, and dignitaries that included Duke of Kent, Prince Edward, who read the Queen's message for the occasion, invited Heads of State like Olusegun Obasanjo of Nigeria and Ellen Johnson-Sirleaf of Liberia, Busumuru Kofi Annan, immediate past Secretary General of the United Nation and his wife Nane, Dr Gertrude Mongele, President of the Pan-African Parliament, the Reverend Jesse Jackson, the black civil right activist, chiefs members of the Diplomatic Corps, foreign dignitaries, Members of the Council of State, Service Commanders thronged the grounds and erupted into thunderous applause.

"*Ghana, your beloved country is free forever*", Dontoh, said in a voice that sounded very much like Dr. Nkrumah's. This was greeted with thunderous cheers. Not few shed tears of great historic joy. The former President of Namibia, Sam Nujoma was right when he described Nkrumah as a "prophet". Dontoh brought back the memory of the first President, quoting his famous statement: "*Our Independence is meaningless unless it is linked up to the total liberation the African continent.*" Since Nkrumah made this declaration he tireless worked for independence of other countries that included Nigeria and the Congo. There is a sound political wisdom to say that it was not just celebration of Ghana Independence but African Independence.

Mandela - *Long Walk For Humanity*[*]

On Wednesday 18th of July, *Tata* (Father) Nelson Mandela was 89 years old-or *better still* 89 years younger, judging by his ever refreshingly original new ideas on how to help humanity out of the increasingly decadent global power infrastructure (witness his newly formed *Elders' Forum!).* His 700-plus page autobiography entitled *Long Walk To Freedom* is a compulsory reading for every living soul, (regardless of race) thirsty for justice and fairness in an increasingly unjust and unfair world. In the book, so aptly described by Wole Soyinka, the Nobel Prize winner for Literature, as "*...a work of constant revelations*", *Madiba* (as fondly revered) recollected what birthdays meant on the then notorious Robben Island of woes, humiliation and deprivations where he spent 20 years before he was transferred to Pollsmoor Prison on the mainland in 1982. According to him, "Birthday celebrations were bare bone affairs on Robben Island. In lieu of cake and gifts, we would pool our food and present an extra slice of bread or cup of coffee to the birthday honouree." On this totalitarian state of Robben Island, Mandela noted that his 50th birthday was uneventful ("*had passed without notice in 1968*). And that was the great Mandela paradox: every adversity was turned into remarkable advancement. The autobiography so much celebrated and described by Desmond Tutu as "*a fitting monument*" was itself actually conceived and virtually written on the Robben Island. Again according to Nelson Mandela, Walter Sisulu and Kathy, who were fellow inmates on the island, had insisted that the perfect time for Mandela's memoirs was on his sixtieth 60th birthday: "*Walter said that such a story if told truly and fairly will serve to remind people of what we have*

[*] Daily Trust, 30th July 2007

fought and still fighting", Mandela narrated. True to Walter's expectation, this book has proved a worthy text of revelations of Mandela paradoxes. Mandela's Eastern Cape Province, abode of his birth at the turn of the twentieth century, (1918 precisely) consisted of only three huts; *one for sleeping, one for cooking and one for storing food. Each of the huts has been crafted by the hands of the mother; Nosekeni* Fanny. Today, Mandela's living space is a huge global village in which he remains a powerful moral figure with countless "huts" in which former heads of government inclusive of the likes of notable American former living presidents Bill Clinton and Jimmy Carter are co-neighbours.

In an age in which leadership is becoming an endangered specie and even scandalously and shamelessly synonymous with crass corruption (witness Nigeria's Nigerian trial of state governors)! Nelson Mandela has proven that leadership is not just rhetoric but practical actions and words and direct service delivery for humanity.

Besides *Long Walk To Freedom*, my next recommended text on *Nelson Mandela is Leading like Madiba* written by Martin Kalungu Banda. This book is a remarkable story of *leadership lessons* from Nelson Mandela as narrated by anonymous people of humble background. It is an historic collection of reflections of the man of destiny and the extent how he has touched humanity for the better. Two of these reflections are worth recollecting here.

The first leadership lesson from Nelson Mandela deals with sharing the credit of leadership with others. Mandela was asked what was his reaction to the compilation of a CD of his collected greatest speeches on a SABC (South African Broadcasting Corporation) morning live programme. His response is worth being read:

> "Vuyo (the TV presenter) I feel bad because the CD does not give a fair picture of this country's history. You and I know that the greatest of speakers among the men and women that waged the struggle against Apartheid I am not even eloquent". " I would have been happier if my speeches were simply some among the great speeches that were made by our country's eminent personalities such as Oliver Tambo, Chris Hani, Walter Sisulu, among many others. By so doing, we would be painting the right picture of our country's history. ..the reality of our struggle is that no individual among us can claim to have played a great role from the rest."

Mandela's response is recommended for both former President Olusegun Obasanjo and eternally sit-tight President Robert Mugabe about how not to assume that only they and they alone deserve the honour and dishonour of the wealth and ruination of nations (more of the latter!) they preside over.

The second testimony comes from Nomhle, a South African nurse who shows that Mandela while serving as a state President spent a lot time leaning how not to use power while in office compared to Presidents on the continent who spent time using power to bully and oppress. According to the reflection:

> "he practised restraint when he could have used power to settle scores with those who have treated him and his colleagues as if they did not matter. When he was in such a strong position he could push others to comply with him, he prefer to consult, persuade and even plead in order to settle matters. Instead of intimidating people with his power, he chose to bargain and quite often to forgo to forgo the short time sweet victory."

Again tell this story to the *Obasanjos* and *Mugabes* of Africa. Mandela is *just not a servant leader but truly servant-servant.*

By far, the greatest asset of Mandela is his originality. While serving African leaders repeat unhelpful dogma of the old and while the last African union (AU) in Accra Ghana was split between protagonists and antagonists of so- called United States of Africa (USA), Mandela on his 89th birthday offered the world, not just Africa, a refreshing menu of all inclusive global non-racial idea of *Elders Forum* made up of the likes of himself, Jimmy Carter of USA and of course minus "elders" like Mugabes and Obasanjos. Long live Nelson Mandela!!

Fela's *Uncompleted Works*[*]

Yours truly was a witness to the public presentation of the "*complete Release works*" of the legendry Afro beat, Fela Anikulapo Kuti by Femi Esho, the chief driver of *Evergreen Musical Company Ltd (EMCL)*. The event took place at the uptown elitist Muson centre, Lagos in April this year as part of the 10th anniversary of the death of Fela. Fela actually died on 2nd of August 1997 at the age of 59 (1938-1997). A total of 40 volumes of Fela's released works (distinct from hundreds of unreleased) inclusive of Highlife era tunes, spanning three hard working decades were presented to a predominantly elitist audience. The select audience was a radical departure from the classless critical crowd of the late Fela's shrine downtown, at the then notorious Pepple Street at Ikeja. And that is part of the paradoxes of the late great African musical commentator and if you like musical columnist (every of his album dwarfs many present day newspaper columns in critical commentaries!). Eternal credit goes to Fela; the very elite that was part of the conspiracy of action and inaction to undermine his, autonomy, independence and entrepreneurship at the infamous Kalakuta Republic in 1977 through wholesale military invasion was the very elite that was outsmarting each other to "privatize" his legacy. Talking about paradoxes, the occasion was chaired by no less a notable than the Chairman of PPPRA, Chief Rasheed Gbadamosi, a childhood friend (not necessarily a comrade of the legend). Again paradoxically Gbadamosi led agency did much during OBJ's recent lost decade of misrule (1999-2007) to undo every thing that Fela stood for through serial petroleum price increases without sustainable quality products which invariably led to public welfare loss and

---

[*] Daily Trust, 6th August 2007

deepen poverty Anikulapo-Kuti (*The One Who Carries Death in his Quiver!*) decried via his eternal thundering saxophone. This paradox of Fela represents another fall out of another contradistinction of the great Afro-beat King. While Fela unapologetically sang and singularly risked life for the multitude of voiceless of the Africans he offered messages and musical content that transcend the sleath hierarchy, of class, gender or tribe and race. He was truly a global actor in the great traditions of similar artists like South Africa's Mariam Makeba, Hugh Masekela and Senegal's Yusuf Ndoor among great other artists. He acted local (down town Ikeja!) but his thoughts are global in that they resonate in Cape Town, Cairo, New York and London! As a privileged fan of the late philosopher and poet, yours sincerely is even further privileged to have 40 volumes of Fela's audio CDs (about 240 tracks of woven danceable words) in my collection of great ideas and thoughts of twentieth and twentieth centuries. However the point cannot be overstated that Fela's works are far from being completed in the sense of commercial orientation of producers and marketers alike. Fela sang for *change, change and change.* For as long as that desired change proves elusive in his country, Nigeria, Fela's works are far from being completed and possibly inexhaustible. On the contrary, Fela's rude messages about underdevelopment with the hope of inspiring radical changes for development have fallen on the deaf ears of dealer-rulers of the recent past such that the witty wag's messages have to be repackaged in modern day noisy raps for our new set of *servant-leaders.*

For instance in the 1970s at a time it was not fashionable to patronize Africa and even more fashionable to ape Europe and America, Fela sang *Buy Africa.* His contention was that prosperity would elude Africa without patronage of its products and ideas by Africans. Over 30 years after that rude awakening, Nigeria had uncritically enlisted in the World Trade Organization (WTO), a club of trading nations without products to trade but with multiple dumped products to buy. The result today is that Nigeria has become a huge market for dumped products from Europe and China leading to factory closures, unemployment and poverty true to Fela's foresight. Fela's *Tears, Sorrow and Blood* in the late 1970s was seen then as danceable lyric which aptly summed up his tragic first hand "treatment" in the hands of the military tormentors. Today we all saw that singular track as a powerful reminder of the legacy (*regular trade mark!*) of military dictatorship. Yet it is far from being over. Just as Fela sang, in that historic ode to dictatorship, his people (Nigerians!) are still in *fear to fight for justice, freedom and liberty* such that we were under the heels of majority thieving governors, for eight years (they even rented cowardly cheap crowd to hail them in prisons!). *Sorrow, Tears and Blood* remain regular trade marks from the trails of armed and unarmed robberies to the official and street kidnappers of Niger Delta creeks. Fela's works are certainly far from being over!

Follow-Follow is a classical warning against dependency and neo-colonialism. Fela urged that we *open sense, open eye and open brain* as we are susceptible to received wisdom. He observed that in the books of received wisdoms lie *termites, cockroaches and rats* as distinct from the promised sweet outcomes of the salesmen and women of received ideas. Today three decades after Fela's prophetic warning, Nigeria is spell bound with received ideas from the *books* of Bretton Institutions, namely IMF and World Bank. The results included Nigeria's willingness to pay from first charge London and Paris Clubs $30 billion dubious debts while it owns its senior citizens (pensioners!) some N2.6 trillion and willing to offer bonds in place of cash. The *follow follow* Fela decried has landed us in the pit of poverty and corruption competing on the UN Human Development Index with the likes of Sierra Leone, Malawi and Cameroon! Nigeria was a *Big, Blind Country* (*BBC*) such that only Fela knew that *Zombie no go go unless you asked am to go*! Fela shares part of the credit of the global democratization process and the attendant struggle and sacrifices that trailed it in the 1980s. He knew from painful personal experience that we must eventually confront dictatorship as we later did for dictatorship knows only *one way* that was the way of *Zombie.*

The theme of 2006 UNDP Report was; *Beyond scarcity: Power, poverty and global water crisis.* This Report showed that water and access to water by majority of people is indispensable to any serious effort at meeting the millennium development goals (MDGs). Yet that was what Fela has pointed out in his ever green *Water No Get Enemy*. The sad commentary is that in spite of indispensability of water, it has "enemies" in Nigeria that include 14-year old Miss Musa from Bauchi

State who spoke through an Interpreter at the launch of the Report last year. According to her, she spent hours in the morning and at night looking for water that is not available in her community which explains why 14-year old is not literate enough to address the President Olusegun Obasanjo in English at the Yar'Adua Centre. That event which did not hit the headlines like other partisan events at the centre graphically brought home the pointed disconnection between the huge budgetary allocations to water resources and abysmal lack of access to safe water in Nigeria. Precisely because Nigeria cannot make clean water available for its citizens or make its citizens 'enemies' of water contrary to Fela's universally acclaimed insight that *water no get enemy*, we can hardly say his works are completed. The challenge is for those who dare to carry on where the legend stopped, *sorry*, where he had *a short break*. "*Fighters never say good bye*"! Gracia Machel, *widow of Samora Machel and Nelson Mandela's wife* put it better in a dedication to her husband (Samora Machel) brutally shot down by cowardly racist South Africa in 1986. Long Live Fela's uncompleted works!

Sunday Awoniyi: A Day After*

Blessed are the dead,
For they will;
Never be suspected...
- *BM Themba, a South African poet*

"Monuments Only Attract Pigeons"
- *V. I. LENIN*

Quite significant to note how the death of Chief Sunday Awoniyi made instant newspapers columnists (fifth brand inclusive!) of many Nigerian high and the notables associated with the late *Aro* of Mopa. As a stressed weekly columnist, yours mournfully felt paradoxically instantly relived for once to read (and read) the volume of tributes dedicated to the memory of Chief Awoniyi. What else could regular commentator have said about the dead that have not been eloquently written and said by instant mourners? At the special *Day of Tribute* organized by Arewa Consultative Forum (AGF) on Thursday at the International Conference Centre as well as at his interment on Saturday at his country home; Mopa, everybody of note struggled to be counted. There was almost unity of superlatives and adjectives on the worth and stuff of the late chief such that observers wondered if some of the mourners in search of unity of purpose would not have invented the funeral in the first instance to make a point. The most irresistible assemblage of words of mourning (or was it praise singing?) was attributed to the Senate President, David Mark. Even with "heavy heart" witness senate President's tribute:

* Daily Trust, December 17, 2007

> "He (late Chief Awoniyi) was an active a politician, a seasoned technocrat and admirable administrator who rose to the rank of permanent secretary. An affectionate father, a grand father, a community leader and above all a man of peace." "Chief Awoniyi was a principled honest and dedicated Nigerian who lived by example. He epitomised service to the nation. He was one of Nigerian's architects of modern democracy, particularly his unparallel commitment to the tenet of democracy and rule of law."

With "heavy heartedness" that generously threw up such well crafted free-fall praise-prose for the dead your guess is as good as mine what words to expect from senate President when the heart was light enough to do a sober assessment of the *Aro* of Mopa. The critical question however is; must we celebrate life or death or both? It was debatable and even pointedly questionable if the chief was so much honoured with words and presence during his life time as he was revered at grave side. Put in another way, are we enjoined by our faith, the national pledge and Nigeria's Constitution (in-that-order) to whatever reason just honour the best among us (dead or living) with soothing and comforting words (that certainly would not wake up the dead) or to strive to copy their acknowledged best practices. We might inadvertedly be lying about the worth of the dead (Only Allah is the best judge anyway!) if we cannot also dare to say we also stand for all the attributes we ascribe to the dead. I read through all the tributes I could not single out any notable mourner who dared to say I am like Sunday Awoniyi in fearlessness, selflessness and patriotism we claimed he stood for. The only tribute that approximates my expectation was that of President Musa Yar'Adua who dared to offer himself for critical assessment when he said: "I will emulate the late elder statesman by giving Nigerians purposeful, selfless and committed leadership." Even as significant and radical as President's graveyard tribute to Chief Sunday Awoniyi was (which explained the thunderous ovation that greeted it!) the President's was still a promissory note. Until this promise translates into reality, nobody should ever say we truly missed the departed statesman. In fact most mourners were shamelessly cheeky to compare him to the great past heroes accepting approri that today, national heroes are endangered species. Just witness this shameless leap to the past: "He (Awoniyi) walked the path of "timber and calibre" like Sir Ahmadu Bello, the Sardauna of Sokoto, the late Zik of Africa as well as Chief Obafemi Awolowo." Are we saying that there was nobody among the multitude of notable mourners worthy of emulation? We say Awoniyi was the disciple of Sardauna, pray whose disciples are we? Chief Awoniyi was an acknowledged and celebrated Sardauna's follower; pray who dares to be Awoniyi follower in words and deeds? Yours sincerely is conscious of the dictum that we dare not say anything bad of the dead which might have explained why we fell over each other to out-praise the dead. But there is no known saying that we the living should accept our gross shortcomings that we stood for nothing as much as late Chief Awoniyi stood and actually died in the cause of that something, however controversial. Until we resolve this contra-distinction, all the tears so far only filled hypocritical basket thus self serving, the same official cancer Awoniyi fought to the last. The South African poet, B.M. Themba, was right to have observed that "Blessed are the dead, (including Awoniyi) because they (the dead) will Never again be suspected". It is we the living that should be suspected of mourning words said but not believed, tears shed that are not real, mourning that resembled home video rather than the reality of Nigeria's governance crisis.

A critical look at the collection of notables at Awoniyi graveside revealed a mix-bag of our divisive and conflictual lot; from politicians to businessmen and women. It shows that in the final analysis we can actually find a common purpose if we must. The question is: a day after Chief Awoniyi's burial are we going to find the necessary unity to put an to poverty, power outages, corruption, election rigging, unemployment and all that constitute the existing intolerable underdevelopment amidst the national riches and blessings, the same message that Chief Awoniyi conveyed with candour and remarkable gut?

It is remarkable that of all the commentaries, nobody has interrogated the cause of the death of our so much loved one. Yours sincerely shares the eternal fact that Almighty gives and takes in whatever forms. But we are also enjoined to "work and worship" ala Sardauna for better life and long life. Certainly 75 years was above national life expectancy average of forty-you-know-better. But what manner of a country is it that wastes his elder-statesman at 75 on the road? Ian Smith, the notorious Rhodesian hangman recently died at his hometown in Cape Town at the age of 85 in spite of atrocities he ever committed. Why do we waste the lives of our best performers?

A day after the reported accident that eventually led to the death of the late statesman many have further died in their hundreds in road related accidents.

A day after the chiefs accident 12 unknown lives have been reportedly wasted along Kaduna/Kafachan road.

Also a day after Chief Sunday's burial, 20 lives have been lost along Asaba/Onitsha road. We cannot say that we sincerely mourn Chief Awoniyi if we don't honestly put an end to cheap wastage of human lives, low or high alike. Tears are not just enough for chief Awoniyi, if there are no radical policy changes to ensure good governance that make lives less cheaply wasted.

Gambari's Nation-Building Challenges*

Precisely because yours truly *is involved* (apology to Chief Ojukwu) I bear testimony that Mustapha Akanbi Foundation (MAF) is coming of age. Inaugurated in Ilorin, Kwara State on 12th of September 2006, MAF is adding value in this notorious age of national value-subtractions ($10 billion, sorry, $16 billions on power without power supply!). Out of simple and enduring noble objective to serve as "…a veritable platform for promoting democratic values and fostering sustainable and viable democratic development in Nigeria," MAF within the past activist year has left bold imprints in areas of education, human empowerment, health, anti-corruption campaign and good governance. Apart from significant humanitarian work which has raised hope for the sick and disabled, the Foundation is *catching them young* via reading and writing skill acquisitions in public secondary schools. The Foundation *is acting local but thinking global* through high profile public agenda setting lectures. Its Chairman, Honourable Justice Mustapha Akanbi has commendably come out with sustainable initiative to further continue in retirement same good work spanning some decades at the bar and the bench. The singular commitment, passion and courage of Justice Akanbi manifest in yearly topical themes that elevate public debate from the pedestrian. Last year, the theme was *Participatory Democracy and Good Governance.* Against the background of the on-going pedestrian "debate" about nudity in the national assembly, it was therefore once again refreshing that MAF last Thursday elevated national discourse through the timely theme: "Challenges of Nationhood and Good Governance".

* *Daily Trust* (Monday, February 11, 2008)

This year's lecture entitled the "Challenges of Nations Building: The Case of Nigeria" was ably delivered by Professor Ibrahim Agboola Gambari, Under-Secretary-general and special adviser to the UN Secretary-General. He rightly indicated that his views are not that of UN. Nonetheless, the shared thoughts for food are consistent with global best thoughts on good governance long advocated for by the UN. Again assuming those that are paid to make a difference in our worsening plight are reading?

First, Professor Gambari commendably brought to the fore, the increasingly endangered notions of nation-hood and nation-building. No country has uncritically embraced the myth of globalization than Nigeria. On the one hand, Nigeria's master-leaders (or are they servant-leaders?) had demonstrated more confidence in "foreign investment" rather than creatively unbundling the latent huge domestic energy for growth and development. Former President Olusegun Obasanjo uncritically spent more time ostensibly wooing investors than concentrating on cultivating and building critical institutions of nation building that would make investment, (foreign or local) to thrive. Since then the nation has been imperilled with collapsed domestic investment and institutional decay. On the other hand, there are also citizens who carry on as if it does not matter if their country exists or not. Gambari reminded the latter, no less than the former that today, there are millions of stateless citizens in the world on account of failed states and collapsed nations stressing the need for Nigerians to renew commitment to nation-building given that the alternatives are simply unthinkable (witness Somalia!) What professor Gambari however diplomatically ignored is the painful truism that many Nigerians are today voluntarily giving up their citizenship for that of other countries, no thanks to failing Nigerian state service delivery. Even today, our own Chinua Achebe is counted as African American making the point that a nation is not just a group of people but well-living secured people. With the highest population of African descent in different part of the world especially in the US the concept of Nigerian nation-hood is problematic. Everybody agrees with Gambari's shared perspective that: "Even in these days of globalization and rapid international flows of people and ideas, having a viable nation remains synonymous with achieving modernity. It is about the institutions and values which sustain the collective community in these modern times." Wealth of a nation is not necessarily in its geographical size or population but in its industry, competitiveness and productivity and above all service delivery. As a foot-ball loving nation, following the disastrous outcomes of the recently concluded Cup of Nations, in which "giant of Africa" crashed out at quarter-final, (even Ghana's 9man team dwarfed Nigeria's 10 man-"team") Nigerians appreciate better that intangibles like football do not rest on the nation's leaders' boisterousness or "inscriptive perspective" of "Giant of Africa" (or is it $100 per barrel nor "excess" crude receipts) but its industriousness and competitiveness.

Secondly Professor Gambari identified critical five nation-building challenges for Nigeria, namely history, socio-economic inequalities, constitutional reforms, institution building and leadership. Two of these challenges, (history and socio-economic inequalities) are of special importance. On history, Professor Gambari reminded us of how colonialism underdeveloped Nigeria via separate regional development which in turn undermined cohesive national development as witnessed in Ghana or South Africa. According to him: "Nigeria never had a central rallying figure like Kwame Nkrumah in Ghana or Nelson Mandela in South Africa. Instead, each region threw up its own champions." But was that really the historic fact? Colonial blame-game almost fifty years after independence is defeatist and diversionary and clearly unhelpful. With not less than five former state governors on trial for alleged trillion naira public thefts and growing demand for accountability on the part of former Presidents, the great African scholar, Guyanese Walter Rodney would have written today on *How Africans underdeveloped Africa* no less than he once reflected on How Europe underdeveloped the continent. Professor Gambari certainly compared like with unlike when he compared Nigeria with South Africa or Ghana in terms of leadership turnover immediately after independence. Today it is fashionable to compare Nigeria with city states like Singapore or Botswana. But the point cannot be overstated that immediate post-Independence Nigeria was as formidable as newly independent Ghana and South Africa. In fact no comparison with South Africa because it was Tafawa Balewa government, within the OAU that helped in setting the process of liberation of South Africa a process that did not consummate until 1990. Zik of Africa, Sir Tafawa Balewa, Chief Obafemi Awolowo and late Sir Ahmadu Bello as well as late indefatigable Aminu Kano might be called "regional champions", but they were champions nonetheless with significant equal status and prominence like Nkrumah or Nelson Mandela. I would rather say that Nigeria once had many "Nkrumahs" and "Mandelas". Better put, it is other countries that could not throw up regional developmentalist leaders like Sardauna, Awolowo and Aminu Kano. Nigeria's strength was others' weakness. With benefits of insight that history offers, Nigeria recorded significant growth rate during the tenures of these "regional champions" than the misrule of subsequent modern charlatans. All the industrial estates these regional leaders built have been replaced by churches, leaving the roads with Okada riders and mass of under-employed and unemployed. Regional competition of the old for space for value addition in manufacturing and agriculture has been crudely replaced by state competition for grafts and corruption. Chinua Achebe could not have written that "*the problem with Nigeria was leadership*" during the tenure of these regional leaders as he eventually did during the misrule of "national" leaders in the 1980s. The challenge of history for Nigeria is to start from where these regional leaders left us rather than dismissing them as local champions. Nigeria is in dire need of champions, local and federal and if what we had before was seen as local champions all we need is giant leap backward.

The challenge of socio-economic inequalities tasks the imagination of state governors and federal government alike. Professor Gambari rightly noted that,

> "an important aspect of nation-building is the building of common citizenship. But how can we have a common citizenship when the person in Ilorin has a radically different quality of life from the person in Yenagoa? Or when the woman in Gasau is more likely to die in childbirth than the woman in Ibadan? Through the development of the economy and equal opportunities for all, or through the development of social welfare safety nets, mature nations try to establish a base-line of social and economic rights which all members of the national community must enjoy. Not to enjoy these socio-

economic rights means that the people involved are marginalized from national life."

The bane of regional/state differentiation of socio-economic opportunities however is that it rests on a false assumption that national socio-economic opportunities abound and that the challenge is that of ensuring equity in distribution. The bitter reality is that no material difference between Ilorin and Yenagoa or Gusau. Nigeria is the only oil-producing country that has consistently featured in the lower rug of UNDP Human Development Index in the past decade. What socio-economic equality do you desire in the context of wholesale national meltdown of power supply, education and health services? Unhelpful regional differentiation between common poverty as distinct from commonwealth must give way to frontal attack on current national underdevelopment, retrenchment of corruption agenda and urgent enthronement of development agenda on a national scale.

Shehu Yar'Adua: Ten Years After*

If there was no national programme of Commemoration for the 10th Year remembrance of the late General Shehu Musa Yar'Adua, *Tafida* Katsina, the seemingly atomised, divided and conflictual comrades and associates of the late politician would certainly have invented one. There can hardly be any other platform in recent times which could possibly accommodate political combatants like former President Olusegun Obasanjo, his Vice President Atiku Abubakar and Chief Tony Anenih (in-that-order-conflict) if not Shehu Musa Yar'Adua Foundation! Not even a reconciliation meeting for Shehu's associates could have been so voluntarily well attended in relatively measured decorum (never mind the star-words). It could not have been imagined that former President Obasanjo and his Deputy Alhaji Atiku could turn a photo-journalist delight competently captioned "*warring and smiling*". Political observers noted that with all his open worries (from PDP convention fiasco to independent power contracts scandals) former President Obasanjo looked more political relaxed at the remembrance lecture, so it seemed! Whatever is said of the late Yar' Adua legacy, it is to the eternal credit of the late General that, ten years after his brutal murder by Abacha dictatorship, he post-humously still serves as a *centre* that prevents *things from falling apart* and indeed shattering into smithereens in his political dynasty. What war of political/partisan attrition of recent times has turned asunder, Shehu's remembrance has somehow put together during the weekend. The late Shehu had many parts which have been well studied and documented, namely as a soldier and civil war hero, a public Servant, a politician and indeed a prisoner who eventually died

* *Daily Trust* (Monday, March 10, 2008)

a hero. Of all his many worthy acknowledged attributes, *Shehu-the-politician* captured national and international imagination. Indeed it was his political involvement which climaxed in his patriotic and courageous ultimatum to Abacha to quickly democratise the nation that landed him in the maximum dictator's prison and eventual death. Thus, in assessing Yar'Adua's relevance ten years after his death, a critical look at the nation's political landscape comes handy. The question is: How has the nation fared politically since 1997, Shehu died in Abakaliki prison after eighteen months incarceration?

Paradoxically, answer to this question is not far fetch. Answers are contained in the star-words of the political associates turned combatants at the historic lecture. Again thanks to the late Shehu for living an imprint worthy of annual reflection that once attracted global leaders like Nelson Mandela and late Benazir Bhutto as speakers. The annual reflections are being ably, tirelessly and quietly coordinated by Yar'Adua Foundation's Director General Jacqueline W. Farris. A content analysis of the tributes made by the late politician's associates and comrades at his 10th remembrance lecture ably delivered by His Excellency, Paul Kagame President of the Republic of Rwanda will definitely offer some answers as to where Nigeria is politically since 1997 when Shehu died.

When a distressed and depressed politician was called to give an opening prayer at a political function, only the politically naïve should expect a quote from the scripture. Many were therefore not surprised that Chief Tony Anenih turned a prayer session to clearly partisan diatribe. Witness him: "Thank God for the President we have now. We pray that God will give you the courage wisdom and political will to clear the rot you inherited from the previous administration."

Readers are at liberty to disregard Anenih's reference to God and Godliness (he himself did not mean to drag Almighty to what President Umaru Musa Yar' Adua aptly described as "self-inflicted" woes!). But we should note that the Chief, one time Chairman Board of trustees of 8-year ruling party and indeed a Minster of Works has accepted as much that what is at hand is political "rot" inherited from the previous administration. Since Anenih had limitation imposed by prayer session, former Vice President Atiku and indeed former President Obasanjo unwittingly gave definitions of political rottenness in their successive diatribes, tagged tributes to late Shehu Yar' Adua.

According to former Vice President Atiku: "Late Yar'Adua stood for good governance, free and fair elections and does not use power to intimidate anybody, even his opponents, and sees politics as a means of bringing people together for the common good." Given the scandals that characterized 2007 elections and general climate of undemocratic conduct in the country, what Alhaji Atiku meant is that 10 years after Shehu, Nigeria is many steps backward democratically. Indeed by his reference to those who *use power to intimidate opponents, rather than seeing "politics as a means of bringing people together for the common good*", means that the former Vice President said as much that what we had in recent past under OBJ was some *Abachaism* albeit without Sani Abacha! Obasanjo also accepted without saying so that he actually underdeveloped the country democratically in the last eight years, making the Republic more divided and polarized. Witness him: "Yar' Adua unites Nigerians even in death, because here today, there are people who ordinarily would not like to sit together."

Pray if late Shehu united Nigerians even at death, can OBJ say he did as much for the nation politically? What with divided party and endless counting of votes a year after "elections"? If you are still in doubt about where we are ten years after Shehu then read President Umaru Musa Yar'Adua. In his address, President Umaru Musa Yar' Adua listed the daunting challenges facing Africa (read; Nigeria) today to "include poor infrastructure, weak government institutions and structures, resulting from economic and political mis-governance, mindless, corruption, ethnicity, self-service, politics of intolerance, and a lack of commitment to national ideals." So much for Nigeria, sorry, Africa after Shehu Yar'Adua!

By the way did anybody listen to the address of the Special Guest of Honour President Paul Kagame, President of the Republic of Rwanda? According to him, after the genocide Rwanda is now on the march to recovery under the banner of all inclusive Vision 2020 Agenda. He also disclosed that Rwanda has recorded 98 per cent primary school enrolment within the past 10 years. Pray what is the Nigeria's school enrolment rate after eight years of multi-billion naira UBE scheme? The fact that these critical issues which President Paul

Kagame threw up did not feature at all in the serial obscene diatribes of Shehu's political associates shows how ten years after Nigeria is far from issue-based politics.

Mugabe as History*

"The Greater the Visible Order, the Greater the Hidden Disorder"
- Ben Okri, *A Way of Being Free*

Whether he goes for run-off after the inconclusive parliamentary and presidential elections or there is a re-run as dubiously reportedly being demanded by his ruining (sorry, ruling) ZANU-PF, there is no doubt that President Robert Mugabe of Zimbabwe is fast becoming part of unsavoury history like all patriots turned dictators before him. With opposition having as many as 105 seats in the 210-seat parliament, leaving ZANU-PF with 93 seats, nobody should remind Mugabe that the market is empty. When the 84-year old President marked his 80th birthday, he signified willingness (sic) to retire in 2008. Four years after, Mugabe, the man, Zimbabwean opposition media derides as '*Big-Mouth*' is still "active" in Zimbabwe's politics of manipulation and intimidation that made colonial politics of oppression and dictatorship of Ian Smith regrettably comparable.

As this writer reflected when Mugabe was 80, discussing Mugabe puts objectivity on trial. No Head of State has further polarised a distressed continent in recent times as Mugabe. Recently Kenya with its irresponsible politicians nearly made Zimbabwe looked well (at least we have witnessed ethnic cleansing a la Rift Valley!). But events of the recent weeks in Harare confirmed that Zimbabwe remains the weakest link, not necessarily Kenya, in the already weakened democratic chain in the continent. The road Libya's Gadafi increasingly finds thorny is where Mugabe finds smooth. It is either you are '*for*' or '*against*' *a 'liberation fighter', 'a land grabber', 'a dictator'*, ad

---

* *Daily Trust* (Monday, April 7, 2008

infinitum. Yet, as controversial as Mugabe will ever be, we must still come to terms with an African statesman at 84, desperately clinging to power 28 years in power first as a Prime Minister and now as an indeterminate President.

Mugabe's life (political life) seems inversely related with Zimbabwean progress. One time Maoist guerrilla fighter, famous for his African print wear at pre-Independence Lancaster Summit, a man imprisoned for well over a decade, but emerged as post-colonial leader in 1980 now 24 years with three-piece suit (no more African print) has truly come of age. Mugabe has undoubtedly survived and put his imprint on the Zimbabwean map. But how has Zimbabwe fared under his two-decade rule? Zimbabwean dollar was 8 to 1 in 1995, today, it is 6000 to 1 and certainly in some more zeros. Price riot is the norm with the inflation at indeterminate per cent. Unemployment is 70 per cent. The political class is far more bitterly divided than at Independence. His former finance Minister, Simba Makani, is now an opposition challenger. 'Treasonable trials' arrests, draconian laws, detention and persecution of opponents, characteristics of colonial settlers' rule are now common features of Mugabe's Zimbabwe. We may engage in academic sophistry identifying reasons for the forces responsible for today's Zimbabwean decay no less than we may explain why colonial settlers, subdued the African people in the 1890s. Yours truly is not unaware of some of these 'reasons'. One reason is the alleged conspiracy of the gang of three, namely British's Tony Blair, Jack Straw and the American's George W. Bush to strangle Zimbabwe following the land reform that disposed few white settlers and returned land back to the disposed blacks. We are reminded of the 'smart' sanctions, which include the suspension from Zimbabwe of the Common Wealth and denial of Zimbabwe's access to IMF/World Bank aid and credit on the prodding of Britain and USA. Another reason is the 'subversive' and 'disruptive' politics of opposition represented by Tsavangirai's MDC and the confused opposition in general. As alluring as these reasons are, they only explain but do not in anyway invalidate the truism that despair statistics is fast replacing hope in the last decade and half of Mugabe's long rule. The truth of the matter is that Mugabe is fatigued and should honorably find some exist that may be hard to identify. He has certainly run out of creative ideas to move Zimbabwe forward and must necessarily bow out now before Zimbabwe collapses under the weight and the rot of his dictatorial unaccountable rule. It is a sad commentary that a land blessed with notable leaders like Joshua Nkomo, Ndabaningi Sithole, James Chikerema, Josiah Tongogara, Herbert Chitepo, Abel Muzorewa as at Independence is today begging for notable successors, no thanks to Mugabe's long-dated repression of opposition. That unpatriotic rubble-rousers like Tshangirai are would be successors to Mugabe shows the acute disservice Mugabe has done to the continent politically. It is a sad footnote on Mugabe's rule that colonialism threw up more qualitative leaders than Mugabe's rule tolerated. Three decades after, opposition is as mediocre as his dictatorship.

Mugabe's celebrated land reform is belated and diversionary. It was actually Nkomo's ZAPU which first championed land reform by frontally questioning the 1979 Lancaster agreement's ambiguous principle of willing sellers/buyers. Mugabe ZANU's answer was war of attrition in Matabele land, ZAPU's political strong hold with unforgettable brutality of the notorious 5th brigade. Mugabe is one 'liberator' who deployed instruments meant for his enemies against the opposition, made up of his own people. Almost like Saddam Hussein! With all the reported current forceful land seizures, the alleged violence against the white settlers is still nothing compared to the criminal violence in Matabeleland in the wake of Independence in 1980, apparently without opposition (certainly with the support) from UK and America. The latest Mugabe's new mask of a '*Commonwealth conqueror*' (sounds like Idi Amin!) is also deceptive. Since when? The Harare declaration (Mugabe's acid-test) on democratisation in Africa was made in Zimbabwe and not in London with his then enthusiastic support. In 1991, he hosted the Commonwealth dining with the Queen and playing rugby with Australian Prime Minister, Bob Hawke. When Nigeria was suspended from the Commonwealth on account of bad governance in 1995, Mugabe never staged a walk-out in solidarity with Nigeria. But today he expects same solidarity instead of enthroning good governance. There may be conspiracy against Zimbabwe, but conspiracy only germinates on a fertile soil, the type under the heel of Mugabe's bad governance. The point cannot be overstated that the responsibility for food shortages, inflation, and human and trade union rights' violations in the final analysis, is Mugabe's at 80 and *not* necessarily with Britain Blair's, Jack Straw or America's Bush or Queen's Commonwealth.

Who Then Leads Like Nelson Mandela?*

As a Madiba's partisan, yours truly has read every available printed word on the 90th birthday of the greatest global citizen of all times. As undergraduate student activists in the late 1970s and 1980s, we discovered very early Nelson Mandela among other great African liberation fighters like Amilcar Cabral, Nkrumah, Sekou Toure, Lumumba, Julius Nyerere, Murtala Muhammed, as great sources of inspiration in the battle for de-colonization, against imperialism and against the great crime against humanity, Apartheid. Since then, I have joyfully become a proud collector of any available book on the force of freedom that Mandela and others represent. From his collected speeches to wall posters, from his autobiography to colourful illustrations and photo albums, Mandela's collections make a worthy library.

Mandela's birthday celebration is over but just as the celebrations preceded (witness London's Hyde Park 40-000 music fans' concert and the earlier unveiling monument!), so is Mandela discourse continues after 18th of July. As significant as global celebrations of Mandela are (minus Nigeria where hourly celebration of corruption makes us to miss out in the global frenzy over courage, leadership and commitment!), a critical review of commentaries on Mandela at 90 shows a missing link of the leadership lessons of the liberation hero. In fact, most commentaries see Nelson as a unique hero who transfigured from adversity of 27 year-long incarceration to global instant moral power on justice and reconciliation. Significant part of Western media added the "human angle" dimension to the story, completely went personal; interviewed scores of relatives and

---

* Daily Trust, 28th July 2008

grandchildren about what the preferences of the great grandfather at leisure. As useful as birthday gist and drum beating for Mandela are, they offer no answer to the critical question: who leads after Mandela? In any case you can not even pose leadership question when most commentators have not assessed Mandela as leader among others and whose qualities must be compared to others.

Again that is the bane of Mandela discourse; we refuse to contextualize the life and times of the living legend with a view drawing appropriate lessons about how to continue where he retires as he rightly challenged the dancing crowd in UK. Mandela told friends and well wishers in London that:

> "As we celebrate, let us remind ourselves that our work is far from complete. Where there is poverty and sickness, including AIDS, where human beings are being oppressed, there is more work to be done. Our work is for freedom for all. We say tonight, after nearly 90 years of life, it is time for new hands to lift the burdens. It in your hands now, I thank you."

The point cannot be overstated that not long ago that Africa had a fine tradition of popular leadership. The anti-colonial struggles through up scores of popular leaders that included Kwame Nkrumah, Julius Nyerere, Lumumba, Dr Nnamdi Azikiwe, Chief Obafemi Awolowo who in turned provided inspirations for the Mandelas. Indeed Africa had always produced the Mandelas' whose authority flew from the aspirations and wishes of their peoples not rigged elections and coup detats or similar power usurpations. What then are the leadership lessons of Nelson Mandela for Africa?

Reagan: Lest We Forget

The volume, no less than the quality of discourse on Reagan and Reagan years remain a thought for food. Since Clinton's Lewinsky scandal, America has never been served on a daily basis on Nigerian media menu through a massive uncritical overload (sorry; download) of received wisdoms. Lewinsky's affair was understandably about sex which psychoanalyst, Sigmund Freud, long showed to arouse curiosity of humanity. If we recall Ken Sarr and his legendary pages of phonographic report and partisan star wars, global murky pond of sexual quirks which trailed Clinton's sexual relations, sexual affairs and sextual relationships (apology to Clinton who recently reportedly apologised for the 'terrible moral error') seemed logical. It however beats imagination how sobering subject matter of death and funeral of the 40th President of United States elicited so much enthusiastic eulogies in Nigeria press. One writer was eager to impress those who care that he shared a birthday with the 'great American hero'. Thank God we have since left the primitive age of Mongol leader, Mangu Khan (5th century A.D.) during which admirers of the deceased joined their masters permanently in the grave, sharing death days. One columnist was even more daring; recommended a Reagan for Nigeria on the ground of his casual leadership style, share laziness and incapacity for staying power during working days (Reagan reportedly got to office 9 a.m. took a sister and closed 5 p.m.) We are enjoined not to ever speak ill of the dead. But the post mortem exaggeration over Reagan was too exaggerated in some Nigerian media for good and measured feelings among the most discernable living observers. Paradoxically here corpses in thousands arising from communal mayhem or motor 'accidents' are just mere statistics worthy not of our sympathy much less active prompt commentaries.

As a matter of fact, while Reagan was being laid to rest, unrest in Adamawa claimed scores of citizens' lives who were in turn buried unacknowledged by the media and columnists of various hues. In the age of globalisation, Nigerian writers' charity flows from overseas. But, what about Reagan and Reagan years, which elicited such servile ill-informed memorials?

Least we forget, Reagan's heroic traits feverishly sold through the media posthumously cannot be substitute for true heroic deficits we witnessed during his tenure. The truth is that Reagan was only a hero as, what John Paul Saul called in his Doubters' Companion, an 'illusion of leadership' rather than actual desired leadership that touched on humanity for the better. He was produced by American democracy, but more than any democratic leader, he subverted rather than advance the democratic frontiers in USA and beyond. Jimmy Carter liberalism was dogmatically trampled underfoot by Reagan rabid anti-communism and market fundamentalism. In mid-eighties, he abolished the 'fairness doctrine' of the federal communications Commission requiring airing times for dissenting views, replacing voice popular with voice establishment. This singular narrowing of expression space contributed to voters' apathy from which America is yet to recover. Jimmy Carter attempted to rescue disillusioned citizenry through promotion of human rights and affirmative actions to uplift the blacks. We then saw the emergence of the likes of Andrew Young as Ambassador to the United Nations and Patricia Harris as Secretary of Housing and Urban Development. Conversely Ronald Reagan reversed this humanistic process, turned Carter's doctrine that law should not be used to protect the rich upside-down. In fact the law was bastardised under Reagan to promote conservatism and the hated status quos. To this extent both Reagan and Bush Presidency appointed more than half of 837 federal judges who are well known right wing justices known for controversial positions on races and women. The worst distortion was the myth that Reagan ended the cold war. The President who once joked that he was 'bombing' Soviet Union could not be said to be cold war weary. Lest we forget Reagan initiated the failed star-wars, which almost put humanity on the prescipe of nuclear disaster. His administration also recorded contra-gate and invasion of Grenada.

About the much taunted Reaganomics, Lance Kirkland, had this to say; it '…is known as the carrot-and-stick policy: for the rich, the carrot; for the poor, the stick." The African Head of States who attended Reagan's funeral must have shared the spirit of South Africa's *Ubuntu* according to which we are all human only through the humanity of other human beings. Reagan was not only Africa blind but 'visited' the continent through the bombing of Tripoli. Above all, at a time Apartheid was declared as a crime against humanity by UN, Reagan and Thatcher were fuelling the despicable system through the notorious policy of constructive engagement. It takes the spirit of forgiveness (or is it forgetfulness?) for any African Head of State to attend Reagan's funeral just as it will be nice seeing George Bush attending Bin Ladin's funeral. For all they care, Ancient Egyptians knew what wealth they expended to accompany their Pharaohs to their tombs but what they least forget were the misdeeds of the Pharaohs.

Essential Obama*

True to expectation, the candidature of Barack Obama for the presidency of United States of America on the platform of Democratic Party, has elicited some sorts of *the good, the bad and ugly* reactions in Nigeria. The good dimension deals with the excitement about the prospects of a candidate of some African ancestry, becoming the first CEO of the most powerful corporate country on earth (*at least if Nigerians can vote*). It is remarkable therefore seeing Nigerians of varying hues (high and low) eagerly preparing for November Uncle Sam's polls, (not next door Ghana's in December) even when their own votes in 2007 polls are still being counted in courts with sundry dubious judgements! American poll has instantly proved a therapy for INEC's serial electoral disasters at home. Nigerians have forgotten that with the best of expressions of interest, their votes will certainly not count either in US November polls. Obama's ascendancy has inadvertently brought to the fore the old received wisdom according to which blood (even in Obama's diluted content!) is thicker than water. Significantly too, Obama candidature is a handy life-time public relations stint for America, such that (some cynics say) Obama could have been "invented" anyway assuming he does not exist! Yours sincerely is averse to conspiracy theory but mindful of it nonetheless. Time will tell if indeed Obama was a Jewish/Republican invention to undermine the Clintons whose position on Middle East are not as servile as Obama's. An indisputably open knowledge however is the sudden emergence of a benign and even a romantic view of the Empire since Eddy Murphy's "*Going ToAmerica*" or something close to that. America was once with the clay of feet. No thanks to intolerable human trafficking called despicable slavery, century long civil rights violations, "*constructive engagement*" with Apartheid South Africa (America never officially

* Daily Trust, 18th August 2008

demanded for the release of Nelson Mandela from prison), Ronald Regan's promotion of brawls as distinct from brain in global governance, (remember Star-Wars that put humanity on the brink of nuclear holocaust?) and serial bombings in Iraq from civilization to stone age. Today, America is now perceived as a land of unfettered opportunities; liberty and freedom which has made a third generation African American immigrant have a short at the Presidency. Thanks to successful candidate Obama.

In Nigeria however the danger is that a legitimate excitement virus is gradually being transmuted into some high profile absurdity flu pandemic which calls for some urgent intervention and indeed explanations about the dynamics and relevance of Obama phenomenon. Take for instance, the feverish/bullish activism of Ndi Okereke-Onyiuke-led Nigeria Stock Exchange (NSE) desperately raising unsolicited funds for the campaign of Senator Obama. The only pedestrian thing comparable to this high level idle drama was watching some miscreant *area* youths carrying the banner of *Bin Laden* in the wake of tragic September 11 claiming what they know obviously nothing about. Paradoxically Barack Obama himself wrote in the *Audacity of Hope* (a compulsory reading!) that a notorious smear media campaign derided him as "Osama Obama". Typical of his confidence and faith in his resolve, patriotism and love of America, Obama would encourage us to "have fun" with such "constant vitriol" which "can wear on the spirit" but the Nigeria's version of the absurd cannot be ignored. Fund for Obama here is at best politically opportunistic and politically corrupting no less that it is ill-informed, naïve, irresponsible and clearly pedestrian.

In fairness to Professor Okereke and her team, their partisan charity started long at home. But experience in absurdity does not make it less absurd. It only makes it dangerous. Somebody offers a joke that if the expected rate of return is right they may soon raise money for Cameroon to consummate the take over of Bakassi! It would be recalled that in 2003 under the banner of *Corporate Nigeria,* the same crowd linked with capital market actually laundered money in billions of Naira for Obasanjo/Atiku Campaign fund in a less than transparent way (we are yet to know who gave what and why?). It is not clear what the rate of return on that singular controversial partisan investment was for its promoters. But chroniclers of that age of money impunity would certainly be unanimous to conclude that the corporate and financial recklessness of OBJ era which led to state promoted investment cronyism vehicle like *Transcorp* had its root in that undue monetization of electoral process boisterously openly backed up by corporate chieftains like Okereke and her crowd. It is self-evident that they learnt no lessons from that controversial partisan scandal at home which explains another attempt at globalizing political mediocrity and *money-miss-road mentality* world wide.

Arising from this corporate indulgence is the conceptual crisis about Obama and his politics and the attendant sheer exhibition of political illiteracy on the part of some of his supporters in this part of the world. If you listen to his spoken words and read his printed inspiring words, certainly Barack Obama emerges as a proud African-American. He unapologetically exhibits *"Africa-ness*" in the face of provocative interrogation of his "genuine" American credentials by adversaries and in spite of his own acknowledgment of the "irresponsibility" (his own word) of his Kenyan father, Harvard trained who nonetheless callously abandoned him, just two years old to single parentage of a compassionate "loving" (his word) white mother, white grandmother, "remote" Indonesian stepfather. The point cannot be overstated. Obama candidature is more than *race* as we parochially see politics here in this part of the world. He is not another *brother* for dubious brotherhood sake (in our corrupting see-nothing wrong *parapo* unhelpful village mentality). Essential Obama is an embodiment of hard and smart work, community work as distinct from private agenda, decent work agenda as opposed Casualisation/down sizing, friendship and love as distinct from "US" versus "Them" Berlin Wall, critical engagement as opposed to cronyism, knowledge capital as opposed to money capital/ money laundering, universal as opposed to race- appeal, family values and faith as opposed to materialism, compassion as opposed to self-aggrandizement, bi-partisanship as opposed to cash-based fund raising mono-partisanship, patriotism as opposed to dependency, and remarkable mix of compromises and pragmatic alternative reformist proposals for global democracy, international cooperation and peace.

Obama defeats the Clintons, Billary, they are called (who in their own right are "African" given their passion for the continent-Bill Clinton is indeed the first colour-blind "African American" President!). Hillary Clinton actually garnered support from front line Black caucus one-time presidential Democratic contender like, Reverend Jesse Jackson. We need explanation beyond colour and tribe to appreciate Obama's multiple identities and his remarkable global appeal as well as his success over colour blind entrenched formidable forces. Obama is truly a new American (note: American!) that stands on all the delicate cutting edges of the divide of the American murky politics. It is unhelpful to own him via silly tribal fund raising project from Africa that in itself begging for ownership of some kind. Witness Obama on race: "An emphasis on universal, as opposed to race-specific, programmes isn't just good policy; it's also good politics."

Nigeria's *busy body* which gathers millions of scarce Naira in the name of Obama seems bereft of Obama's politics and his perspective on Africa. Obama must be alarmed that in a country in which as many as 70 percent are living less than a dollar per day and in which according to him, mosquito nets cost just 3 dollars but still priced beyond the reach of critical mass, some enlightened chieftains of critical institutions of development like Nigeria Stock Exchange (NSE) are selling "affirmative actions" advertised tickets in his name that cost as much as ₦275, 000 ($2,750) per individual and ₦2.5 million (($25,000) for corporate bodies. America's National Democratic Conventions dinner prices which Obama himself finds exclusive are less prohibitive compared to Nigeria's dubious dinners' price list. The fund raisers here can certainly not be holier than the Pope. Obama politics with respect to Africa (which I hail!) is that of "*tough love*" according to which we must demand accountability from our governments and corporate institutions as well as individuals. Interestingly Nigeria is one of the countries he singled out as centre of double standards which manifest in "two legal systems" and again in his own words, "*one for foreigners and elites and one for ordinary people trying to get along.*" Nigeria's Electoral Commission ordinarily should call the so-called "*Africa for Obama 08*" (nothing African about them!) obscene fund raisers to order, assuming the INEC is not part of the new rigging process of Obama campaign. The burden is on Candidate Obama. He has the singular responsibility to reject feverish hot money from the continent that is down but seemingly almost out. He should ask the "do-gooders" to at least "*adopt a public school*" (public schools are as abandoned here as the pupils themselves.) Or better still, he should encourage these Samaritans to follow the footstep of his father-in-law, Frasier Robinson, who earned the love of his children including his wife Michelle, "not through fame or spectacular deeds (like fund raising!) but through small, daily, ordinary acts" (like helping the multitude in need in Ajegunle). In the alternative, Barack should demand from his African supporters for policy initiatives that would deepen his proposals on Africa with respect for market access as opposed to aids and handouts advance Clinton's AGOA further beyond 2009 and build on George Bush's support fund for fight against the scourge of HIV/AIDS among others.

In Praise of Dr Lasisi Osunde (I)*

This coming Friday, the remains of former General Secretary of Nigeria Labour Congress (NLC), Dr Lasisi Osunde will be laid to rest in the ancient city of Benin Edo state. Dr Osunde was the General Secretary of the NLC between 1981 and 1993, well over a decade. Born on the 28th of July 1928 to the respected family of late Adams Osunde and Alimotu Guobadia, Osunde was an embodiment of enhanced human capital through training and retraining that consummated in Phd in political economy at the prestigious Friendship University in Moscow in the former USSR. He was a student participant at the prestigious National Institute for Policy and Strategic Studies, Kuru Jos in 1985 (Course 5). He died on 28th of August 2008 at the age of 80. A dedicated family man; he is survived by his wife, Dr Mrs Adezuwa Safu Lawani-Osunde and four children.

Today we are encouraged to mourn the death of a comrade, an organizer, a father, a principled fighter and negotiator a nationalist and a patriot as well as an internationalist at a time globalization was not as fashionable. Many in life are motivated to join the bandwagon of the great struggle for justice. But very few actually have the *staying power* spanning almost four decades of resistance, persecution and perseverance as the late General Secretary. Dr Lasisi Osunde shared these noble uncommon qualities with departed working class fighters like Alhaji H. P. Adebola, Gogo Nzeribe, Adio Moses, Amstrong Ogbonna, Mpamungo, Wahab Goodluck and, of course, Michael Imoudu.

Osunde left worthy legacies that can and must make books for future generations. Dr Osunde was the General Secretary of the Congress at the special period in Nigeria. The period: 1981 to 1990 was characterized by brutal military dictatorships, labour repressions and labour resistance, economic revisionism (SAP) and mass poverty

* Daily Trust, 22nd September 2008

and struggle for democratization. During this period, Dr Osunde-led Secretariat of NLC under the presidency of Ali Chiroma lived up to the challenge of defence workers' rights offering leadership which collectively head-on engaged military dictatorships at the risks of arrests, detention and oppression. These struggles recorded some state defeats but also significant labour successes that continue to propel the current labour resistance in the country.

One thing that was constant was his uncompromising commitment to the defence of the integrity, autonomy and independence of NLC against state/employers sponsored characters and defence of public welfare.

In July 1986 Babangida military government formally spelt out the main elements of its Structural Adjustment Programme (SAP) which include Naira devaluation, mass retrenchment, petroleum subsidy removal, and wage cuts among others. NLC prepared for a struggle aimed at preventing the erosion of gains which they had won over the years while the regime displayed a determination to push ahead with the programme. Paradoxically the regime promised to take on board the views of the citizenry and respect the human rights of the people in marked contrast to former Buhari's policy of refusing to give audience to labour leaders. However, the regime's blueprint for Nigeria's economic recovery included a continuation of the wage freeze unilaterally introduced by the Buhari regime. This outraged labour leaders who in turn put forward a five-point demand in which they called on the government to: discontinue all negotiations with the IMF for a loan, un-freeze workers wages; end the retrenchment of workers and reinstate those that were sacked by the Buhari regime; pay, in full, the wages and benefits of reinstated workers; and return to collective bargaining in industrial relations. Even though the regime saw labour's demands as 'militant' and 'unreasonable' and brought to bear all pressures to break labour solidarity, it is to the eternal credit of NLC that it got concessions from the maximum rulers. The regime was forced to declare a national debate on the desirability of involving IMF in the country's adjustment process. The NLC presented a major policy document which enumerated the kinds of hardship the IMF and its conditionalities would impose on the generality of Nigerian. The congress called for a total rejection of the IMF loan and campaigned vigorously against the Fund at a time when many Nigerians were suspicious and rightly too, that the regime had all but decided to conclude a deal.

While the national debate on the IMF was going on, the Babangida regime decided to declare a state of national economic emergency that involved cut in wages and salaries of all workers in the public and private sector as well as those of the officers and men of the armed forces by between two and fifteen per cent with effect from 1 November 1985. The emergency was to last for 18 months after which workers would be entitled to a refund of the amount cut from their wages and salaries. Given that the wage increases conceded to workers during the 1982 wage negotiations between the government and the NLC had, by 1985, been eroded by spiralling inflation, labour leaders rejected the deductions announced by Babangida in his broadcast. On 5 November 1985 the NLC under Ali/Osunde gave the government a 21-day ultimatum to rescind its unilateral and undemocratic decision or face a nationwide industrial action. The face off further led to a situation that government was made to listen to NLC. On 21 November 1988, barely four days to the expiry of the ultimatum, the federal government agreed to consider the NLC's demands which included an end to retrenchment, the removal of tax on gratuity and pension, the extension of the pay cut to private sector employers and the pursuit of sound economic policies to revitalise the economy.

The next major battle of the NLC came through the 1986 budget. The government reduced the "subsidy" on the price of petroleum products by 80 per cent thereby further fuelling a hyper-inflationary situation. The freeze on wages was also retained. In the face of the additional hardship which the budget meant for workers, the NLC under the leadership of Osunde renewed its agitation for the lifting of the wage freeze. Numerous pamphlets were issued by the congress and numbers of rallies were addressed by labour leaders to mobilise the working people for a sustained campaign against the government's economic policies.

The principled stand of Dr Osunde-led Congress also manifested when NLC clashed with the government when some students of Ahmadu Bello University (ABU), Zaria, were killed by policemen during a demonstration. The NLC under Osunde declared its solidarity with the students and called for the immediate removal of Vice-Chancellor Ango Abdullahi and the Kaduna State Police Commissioner as well as the trial of the policemen responsible for the fatal shots. The NLC also called on its members to take part in a peaceful precession as a symbolic gesture of workers' outrage at the shootings and solidarity with Nigeria students. The government responded by reaffirming an existing ban on all public procession. Police commands all over the country were put on alert while the State Security Service (SSS) arrested a number of prominent labour leaders. The NLC secretariat was once again placed under siege by a detachment of policemen. The government set up an investigation panel headed by retired Major-General Emmanuel Abisoye to establish the root causes of the ABU crisis. The Secretary-General of the NLC, Lasisi Osunde, was asked to serve on the panel but the NLC rejected the invitation arguing that so long as Ango Abdullahi was allowed to keep his position as Vice-Chancellor, no useful purpose would be served by the Abisoye panel. As far as the NLC was concerned, the government's refusal to include members of the Academic Staff Union of Universities (ASUU) and a representative of Nigerian students chosen by NANS on the panel meant that it was only interested in covering up the true origins and full extent of the crisis. Instead, the NLC leadership decided to support the separate investigation process which the ASUU National Secretariat had set in motion. When the Abisoye Panel released its report, both ASUU and the NLC insisted that it had engaged only in white-washing exercise. In the aftermath of the Zaria crisis, the government decided to disaffiliate ASUU from the NLC in the belief that the university lecturers union was responsible for radicalising the Congress leadership.

The major show down between labour and government came when towards the end of 1987, the government indicated its intention to raise the domestic price of petroleum on the grounds that the 80 percent subsidy removal carried out in 1986 had been eroded by the massive devaluation of the naira on the government controlled foreign exchange market. The government-owned

Nigerian National Petroleum Corporation (NNPC) sponsored paid but unsigned advertisements claiming that the 'subsidy' on oil was indefensible. The NLC put out counter paid advertisements in the major newspapers arguing against the plan to increase the prices of petroleum products and rejected the NNPC's comparison of prices of petroleum products in Nigeria to those non-oil producing countries. The NLC campaign was successful that government opted for repression, arrest and detention of NLC leaders included Osunde ostensibly for subversion. NLC struggle eventually made the regime to promote fictionalization within the Congress which eventually led to the dissolution of the NLC in 1988. We can only salute the late Osunde for offering necessary leadership for the Congress at a time it was needed. Even though government dissolved the NLC executive council just as Abacha dictatorship later did, NLC today survives all these tyrant regimes. Ever principled Dr Osunde rejected Abacha Greek offer to be the Sole Administrator of PENGASSAN after its illegal dissolution in 1993 with these immortal words: "for over 45 years I have contributed to the building of the Nigerian labour movement. It is therefore inappropriate for me to accept a position which is likely to destroy a movement I have spent my life to build."

Nelson Mandela once observed that: "Men and women of rare qualities are few and hard to come by. And when they depart, the sense of loss is made the more profound and the more difficult to mange." However Mandela who certainly is also a model of "rare qualities" consoles us that from the knowledge of the legacies and achievements of the departed comrades flows some comfort. Long Live Osunde!

In Praise of Dr Lasisi Osunde (II)*

On 5th November, 1985, the NLC under Ali Chiroma/Osunde gave the government a 21-day ultimatum to rescind its unilateral and undemocratic decision or face a nationwide industrial action. The face off further led to a situation that government was made to listen to situation that government was made to listen to NLC. On 21st November 1988, barely four days to the expiry of the ultimatum, the federal government agreed to consider the NLC's demands which included an end to retrenchment, the removal of tax on gratuity and pension, the extension of the pay cut to private sector employers and the pursuit of sound economic policies to revitalise the economy.

The next major battle of the NLC came through the 1986 budget. The government reduced the "subsidy" on the price of petroleum products by 80 per cent thereby further fuelling a hyper-inflationary situation. The freeze on wages was also retained. In the face of the additional hardship which the budget meant for workers, the NLC under the leadership of Osunde renewed its agitation for the lifting of the wage freeze. Numerous pamphlets were issued by the congress and numbers of rallies were addressed by labour leaders to mobilise the working people for a sustained campaign against the government's economic policies.

The principled stand of Dr Osunde-led Congress also manifested when NLC clashed with the government when some students of Ahmadu Bello University (ABU), Zaria, were killed by policemen during a demonstration. The NLC under Osunde declared its solidarity with the students and called for the immediate removal of the Vice-Chancellor Ango Abdullahi and the Kaduna State police

* Daily Trust, Monday, September 29, 2008

Commissioner as well as the trial of the policemen responsible for the fatal shots. The NLC also called on its members to take part in a peaceful procession as a symbolic gesture of workers' outrage at the shootings and solidarity with Nigeria students.

The government responded by reaffirming an existing ban on all public procession. Police commands all over the country were put on alert while the State Security Service (SSS) arrested a number of prominent labour leaders. The NLC secretariat was once again placed under siege by a detachment of policemen. The government set up an investigation panel headed by retired Major-General Emmanuel Abisoye to establish the root causes of the ABU crisis. The Secretary-General of the NLC, Lasisi Osunde, was asked to serve on the panel but the NLC rejected the invitation arguing that so long as Ango Abdullahi was allowed to keep his position as Vice Chancellor, no useful purpose would be served by the Abisoye panel.

As far as the NLC was concerned, the government's refusal to include members of the Academic Staff Union of Universities (ASUU) and a representative of Nigerian students chosen by NANS on the panel meant that it was only interested in covering up the true origins and full extent of the crisis. Instead, the NLC leadership decided to support the separate investigation process which the ASUU National Secretariat had set in motion. When the Abisoye panel released its report, both ASUU and the NLC insisted that it had engaged only in white-washing exercise. In the aftermath of the Zaria crisis, the government decided to disaffiliate ASUU from the NLC in the belief that the university lecturers union was responsible for radicalising the Congress leadership.

The major show down between labour and government came when towards the end of 1987, the government indicated its intention to raise the domestic price of petroleum on the grounds that the 80 percent subsidy removal carried out in 1986 had been eroded by the massive devaluation of the naira on the government controlled foreign exchange market. The government owned Nigerian National Petroleum Corporation (NNPC) sponsored paid but unsigned advertisements claiming that the 'subsidy' on oil was indefensible. The NLC put out counter paid advertisements in the major newspapers arguing against the plan to increase the prices of petroleum products and rejected the NNPC's comparison of prices of petroleum products in Nigeria to those non-oil producing countries.

The NLC campaign was successful that government opted for repression, arrest and detention of NLC leaders included Osunde ostensibly for subversion. NLC struggle eventually made the regime to promote fictionalisation within the Congress which eventually led to the dissolution of the NLC in 1988. We can only salute the late Osunde for offering necessary leadership for the Congress at a time it was needed. Even though government dissolve the NLC executive council just as Abacha dictatorship later did, NLC today survives all these tyrant regimes. Ever principled Dr Osunde rejected Abacha's Greek offer to be the sole administrator of PENGASSAN after its illegal dissolution in 1993 with these immortal words "for over 45 years, I have contributed to the building of the Nigerian Labour Movement. It is therefore inappropriate for me to accept a position which is likely to destroy a movement I have spent my life to build."

Nelson Mandela once observed that "Men and Women of rare qualities are few and hard to come by. And when they depart, the sense of loss is made the more profound and the more difficult to manage." However, Mandela who certainly is also a model of "rare qualities" consoles us that from the knowledge of the legacies and achievements of the departed comrades flows some comfort. May his soul rest in peace!

Tajudeen Abdulraheem: Tribute to Tributes*

He was to Africa what Che Guevara was to South America
- *Dimas Nkunda*

Fighters Never Say Goodbye"
GRACIA MACHEL, after the death of her husband (Samora Machel) President of Mozambique in Plane crash in 1986

"From the tributes I have read and heard about you, I am assured me that YOU ARE LOVED in a BIG WAY!!!!! and your spirit will live on. Fare Thee Well Beloved Brother......"
Fare Thee Well Beloved Brother......
Mary Wandia, OxfamGB, Pan Africa Office on Tajudeen Abdulraheem

Many visible larger-than-life state actors had died in power, regardless of their political persuasions. Death template of active statesmen parades great democrat like America's Joseph Kennedy to Zambia's Levi Mwanawasa and Nigeria's patriot soldier Murtala Muhammed. Grace Ogot, the Kenyan writer sums it up thus: "Death knocks at your door, and before you can tell him to come in, he is in the house with you"! But very few departed state actors with all their oiled network of patronage elicited spontaneous torrent of tributes as the non-state global citizen, Tajudeen Abdulraheem who was laid to eternal rest on last Tuesday, in Funtua, in Katsina State. The printed words posted on the internet are in multiple digits and they are raining in every day. Yes granted that death remains a respecter of no one. But the diversity and spread of mourners and shared grief, in the wake of Taju's death shows that good deeds while we are living

---

* *Daily Trust* (Monday, June 1, 2009)

confer us eternal respect after death, which in turn damns the cold hand of death. It has been one unique globalization of grief! The grieved and (indeed the aggrieved!) include state (diplomats', Ministers, Presidents) and non-state actors alike (trade unionists and civil society activists), Africans and Europeans, men and women alike. Apart from written words, of course, the spoken words of grief are loud enough as yours-in-grief bears witness during his burial and Fidau prayer on Tuesday and, 31st of May, Sunday respectively. Definitely, the unspoken words of the global multitude, struggling to recover from the auto accident which on Africa Liberation Day led to the death of Tajudeen Abdul-Raheem (1961-2009) are better contemplated.

Yours sincerely tries to keep pace with the grief tribute overload, if only to console self for a sudden loss of a dear comrade. Even as we are deeply shocked to sound coherent on the lives and times of Taju, we must not refuse to pay a tribute to multitude of selfless tributes to him.

One recurring theme in most of the tributes from Mauritius to Oxford, Nairobi to Cape Town, Lagos to Addis Ababa is Taju's prophetic admonition while alive: Let's Not Agonize Lets *Organize*. If Taju did not invent that singular wake-up-call revolutionary slogan, definitely he popularized and indeed acted on it on to death more than its author could imagine. Paradoxically we are all agonizing after Taju's death!

Our agony is not because we are unmindful of the fact that addictive agony begets greater agonies. On the contrary, we agonize, precisely because a tragic accidental death (fighters never say good bye!), of a pan African organizer on Africa Day is definitely agonizing. Agonizing Taju's death amounts to a legitimately agony! In any case it took an agonized like the late comrade to know that others agonize over deplorable situation of our continent and the urge to do something about it starting with organizing.

Just witness how Dr Tajudeen Abdul-Raheem in a recent commentary agonized over the painful reality that Millennium Development Goal No. 5–improving maternal health–"is way off target". Outlining the dimensions of the problem he singled out the painful experience of his younger sister, Asmau (better known as

Talatua), "aged 33, who died two hours after delivering her second child, a baby boy whom she never held."

Asmau according to Taju "is among the 500,000 women who die each year as the result of childbirth and pregnancy; it's the No. 1 killer of women of childbearing age in the developing world". And true to his admonition, after arguing that "it is not God's will that children should be brought up without their mothers" he dared us to action to halt maternal mortality through simple organizing (not agonizing efforts!) like letter *writings, funds provisions and skills offer-*

Africa, (Taju lived for 53 years) indeed agonized and (still agonises) over the devastating impact of slavery and colonialism, (witness modern day Visa lotteries!), over dependency in place of independence, (he was born almost at Independence of Africa (read: Ghana), corruption in place of development, dictatorship, in lieu of democracy, poverty alleviation instead of wealth generation, wars in place of solidarity and peace ad ifinitum (almost in that order of agony!).

Precisely because very few like Taju took the risk to shoulder the burden of reinventing a worthy Continent, his sudden eternal exist added to the agony of the remaining standing Pan Africans and patriots alike. Kindly bear witness to some of the expressed agonies:

> According to Agnes Kabajuni, Centre on Housing and Evictions (COHRE) she had never seen him in person "but your face was well implanted in my mind; from the many articles I read about you. You might be gone, but your light will still shine, your voice will still echo in many minds and your pen will never dry."

Vijay Makhan of Mauritius reminisced thus:

> "I have been a keen follower of Taju´s actions and regularly read his postcard in Pambazuka. I shall miss the freshness of his thoughts and critical analysis."

Very few disagree that it takes some organizing which Taju favoured to turn out serial tributes to a worthy friend at such a short time of announcement of his burial making us to return to Taju's message: Let's Not Agonize Lets *Organize*! May Almighty Allah make his grave more spacious than the global space he virtually traversed within a short life span! May his dear wife, Tunisian-born, Munirat, and her two daughters regain the sapped energy to bear the loss. Their agony is our agony!

Ageing like Mandela*

"There is no difference between growing old and living"
- *Kikuyu (Kenya) proverb*

"He who forgives, gains the victory"- *Yoruba (Nigeria) proverb*

The world observed Nelson Mandela's 91st birthday on Saturday, 18th of July. At 91, Mandela is still strong. And that is official. According to his wife, Gracia Machel, Mandela goes to his Foundation office and still wants to get things done on his own. The logic of genealogy is that the old ones are progressively dependent. Undoubtedly, the increasingly frail icon of African liberation and former statesman, affectionately called Madiba, (his clan name), is definitely having a great deal of helping hands true to the calling of old age. But very few in his age bracket yearly offer frail (but ever helping and uplifting!), hands to humanity at their birthdays. At 89, Mandela offered the world, (not just Africa), a refreshing menu of all inclusive global non-racial idea of *Elders Forum* which paraded eminent persons like himself, Jimmy Carter of USA and, of course, minus "elders" like *Mugabes* and *Obasanjos*. Mandela marks this year's birthday with another original challenge to citizens of the world. The theme of this year's celebration, as it were, is 67 minutes for public service:

> "People around the world are being urged to dedicate 67 minutes of their day to volunteer for community service. The number reflects the number of years since Mandela dedicated his life to the struggle for equality in South Africa, as he joined the ruling African National Congress in 1942."

---

* Daily Trust (Monday, July 20, 2009)

The birthday which also marks the inaugural Mandela Day, initiated by his charitable foundation has enlisted Mandela enthusiasts like Oprah Winfrey, a long-time Mandela friend, who pledged their volunteer service for the day/week.

In heeding Mandela's call, President Jacob Zuma of South Africa elected to spend his 67 minutes with a group of elderly citizens. ANC "deployed ministers, members and youth leaders to paint a police station, visit a hospital, plant trees and give clothes to orphans". Are we also willing to age like Mandela? Will Academic Staff Union of Universities (ASUU) mark Mandela's birthday week with a relook at its ongoing legitimate indefinite strike (even if only for 67 minutes!) as part of the community service to promote uninterrupted education in Nigeria? Strike suspension is desirable not because, the Federal government cares as such about the union's time honoured legitimate demands for adequate funding of education and better rate of return on teaching service. If the government cared in the first instance, there would not have been two weeks warning stoppage much less an indefinite shut down. ASUU's difference to Mandela's week, flows from the icon's admonition that education must be uninterrupted even under the despicable Apartheid regime which offered inferior delivery to black majority even as we must insist on quality. So far it is the miserable public (and not Ministers whose children don't patronize these universities anyway) that is hourly agonized with repeated school shut down. Will next week NEC meeting of the union suspend the current action in the spirit of community service Madiba called for at 91st anniversary? I bear witness that ASUU has spared more than 67 minutes for work with relatively low pay and in an underfunded sector. Indeed, those to spare some 67 minutes for public service they are being paid for (as enjoined by Madiba) are Yar'Adua's ministers who increasingly exhibit private indulgence as distinct from community service while in public service. Will the Minister of Education, Dr Sam Egwu resign (if only for 67 minutes!) to pursue community service after devoting much hours (and how much?) to televised wedding anniversary dancing steps fortnight ago?

It is significant to note that it is the world that celebrates the Nobel laureate, Nelson Rolihlahla Mandela, who ranks as an icon with Gandhi and Martin Luther King in recognition of his selflessness, courage and unprecedented sense of forgiveness. Artists such as Carla Bruni and Stevie Wonder performed in New York and Johannesburg at celebratory concerts. Are we truly willing to age like Mandela? The most remarkable leadership lesson from Nelson Mandela's life deals *with sharing the credit of leadership with others.* Asked once, about his reaction to the compilation of a CD of his collected greatest speeches, *h*is response is worth being read:

> "I feel bad because the CD does not give a fair picture of this country's history. You and I know that the greatest of speakers among the men and women that waged the struggle against Apartheid I am not even eloquent". "I would have been happier if my speeches were simply some among the great speeches that were made by our country's eminent personalities such as Oliver Tambo, Chris Hani, Walter Sisulu, among many others. By so doing, we would be painting the right picture of our country's history. ..the reality of our struggle is that no individual among us can claim to have played a great role from the rest."

Nigeria parades "elder" statesmen who daily appropriate glory as well as fortune and common wealth meant for the country? Are they also willing to age gracefully like Mandela?

While as a state President Mandela:

> "spent a lot time leaning how not to use power while in office compared to Presidents on the continent who spent time using power to bully and oppress. He practiced restraint when he could have used power to settle scores with those who have treated him and his colleagues as if they did not matter."

Again tell this story to those who dare to age like Mandela. He is not *just a servant leader but truly servant-servant* of the 20th and 21st which explains while the global lobby is on at the floor of United Nations to declare global Mandela Day.

Last weekend, he reportedly had a surprise attendance at the Seventh Nelson Mandela Memorial Lecture – delivered in Johannesburg by microcredit pioneer Professor Muhammad Yunus. His appearance entranced the audience. "The magic is inescapable: When you see Mr Mandela in a crowd, it is as though his face emits rays of sunlight." His voice lacks the "fury and bitterness" of the anti-

Apartheid days, but it is still the voice changing the world for the better. From HIV/AIDS victims to protest against senseless and criminal Bush's war against Iraq and gentle voice for community service this week. Happy birthday Madiba!

Gani: Non-State Actor of All Times*

Chief Gani Fawehinmi SAN died in the early hours of Saturday, 5th of September in a Lagos hospital marking the eternal exit of one of the remaining Africa's progressive advocates and patriots. As his compatriot and comrade, Femi Falana aptly summarised the great loss, the Chief "finally succumbed to the cancer of the lungs. After fighting the dangerous disease gallantly in a London hospital for the past two years, he recently returned home to wait the final hour."

ONE LOSS, TOO MANY

Gani's death coming on the heal of the burial of Professor Omafume Onoge, radical former sociologist of University of Jos and the death of Dr Tajudeen Abdulrahamn in Nairobi Kenya, Nigeria's progressive community is in long season of deep mourning.

GOOD COMPANY

Many are called. Many are enlisted in the resistance against underdevelopment, bad governance and oppression. But very few actually had the *staying power* spanning almost three and half decades of resistance, persecution and perseverance as the icon of Nigeria's bar. Few indeed paraded a remarkable mix of those identified qualities, namely steadfastness, courage, principled stand for justice, kindness, charity and passion for the voiceless and the oppressed.

To this extent, Chief Gani shared these uncommon qualities of departed and living soldiers of justice and opponents of tyranny. Gani's companionship parades Nelson Mandela, late Oliver Tambo, Samora Machel, late Murtala Muhammed, Malcolm X, Martin Luther

---

* *Daily Trust* (Monday, September 7, 2009)

King Jr, J.F. Kennedy, late Fela Anikulapo-Kuti, Professor Claude Ake, Beko Ransom-Kuti, Guyana Walter Rodney, Frantz Fanon, Amilcal Cabral, late Dr Bala Usman, Michael Imoudu, Ghana's Kwame Nkrumah, late Alao Aka Bashorun, Dr Mahmud, Dr Lasisi Osunde among others. Chief Gani was in the class of selfless global citizens like Mahatma Ghandi, Indira Ghandi, Che Guevara, Fidel Castro, and Mother Teresa who opted for discomfort in defence of humanity.

Nelson Mandela once observed that: "Men and women of rare qualities are few and hard to come by. And when they depart, the sense of loss is made the more profound and the more difficult to manage." However Mandela, living icon of *rare qualities* consoles us that from the knowledge of the legacies and achievements of the departed comrades flows some comfort for the living comrades.

UNBEATABLE LEGACIES

What then are the legacies of the late Chief Gani Fawehimi? Very few took so much risk and mobilised all they had including their lives for the sake of others. He once said he often packed his luggage ever ready for detention and operated as if there was no tomorrow. That was at the height of pointed military dictatorship which Gani frontally and almost single handedly confronted with enormous sacrifices including torture and detentions.

DIFFERENT METHODS BUT CONSTANT OBJECTIVE

For Gani the methods and strategies might vary, but the objective is the same: get justice for the oppressed.

RULE OF LAW

Nobody in Nigeria's history has made effective use of instrumentality of the law to push for respect for human rights and good governance as Gani did. President Yar'Adua commendably mainstreams the rule of law against the background of serial impunities of his predecessor.

But as an activist non-state actor, that was what Gani had been struggling for decades. Gani feverishly worked through the rule of law. Yar'Adua only legitimises it. Paradoxically the very same "rule of law" was used to persecute him. He had been in and out of prisons with the frequency that no activist had beaten: Kaduna Prison, (1969) to Nigerian Prison, Bauchi 1996.

ABIDING FAITH

To his eternal glory, those persecutions only strengthened his faith in the judiciary, rule of law and not less. Gani's frustrations and despair about Nigeria's persistent under-development captured imagination. He is often dubbed "fiery lawyer" by the media. The media perception and characterization conceals a methodical hard working systematic and consistent mindset who had won landmark cases which had amended our constitution more than the national assembly could.

LAND MARK CASES WON

The former Head of State, General Muhammed Buhari had tasked us to dig into the archive and bring to the fore the litigations of this great Nigeria's litigant. Chief Gani's dogged fight and litigation against INEC reaffirmed the constitutional right to freedom of association which led to the registration of more political parties thus freeing Nigerians from the political regimentation of INEC. In defence of Nigeria Labour Congress (NLC) (without kobo), he got damning judgement which reaffirmed the workers' right to strike when OBJ administration was bent on criminalizing strikes in the wake of the mass protest against serial fuel price increases by the regime. He insisted everybody including trade unions should obey the laws even as he was eager to evacuate obnoxious judicial pronouncements on behalf of the unions.

RIGHT TO BE DIFFERENT, THERE IS ALTERNATIVE TO EVERYTHING

Gani's spared no one when it came to his commitment to see his convictions through. In 1984 he dared the NBA and appeared before military tribunal to defend corrupt public officials. NBA establishment disowned Gani, but it could not fault his arguments that defence of human rights is not divisible. Indeed that battle further underscores the significant position of Gani in the Bar; it did not diminish him in the least as the enemies had designed.

FORMIDABLE NON STATE ACTOR

Gani was a formidable non-state actor who had impacted on quality of lives than many self-style statesmen. A private sector man, Gani canvassed to the last for bigger kinder and just government. He audaciously demanded that the state should uplift the weak rather than privilege the few. Gani's "undue radicalism" triumphed over conservative rotten theft and corruption regimes of the recent times. The global economic meltdown occasioned by neo-liberal policies of Mrs Thatcher and Ronald Reagan era in the 1980s vindicated Gani's position that the greed of the few would not only deny the needs of the majority but would undermine common wealth in general. The return of bigger state in development through bail outs, stimulus plans and progressive taxation of the rich as well as sanctions for criminal state and market actors such Bernerd Madoff in America, corrupt state officials and bankers in Nigeria reaffirmed the validity of Gani's vision.

PATROTISM AND CITIZENSHIP

Another legacy of Gani is citizenship. At a time it was risky to do so Chief Gani opposed the regime of TINA (There Is No Alternative) that Structural Adjustment Programme (SAP) fostered on the nation. He dared to organize alternative development agenda at the NLC secretariat in mid 80s. He raised the banner of citizenship and patriotism in the face of dictatorship. He was one civilian that put military generals on the edge not with guns but with battle of ideas.

DISINTERESTEDNESS

Very few could be counted on side of selflessness like Gani. He rejected the national award of the Officer of the Federal Republic (OFR) which the Umaru Musa Yar'Adua Administration wanted to confer on him last year.

YAR'ADUA MUST GIVE GANI POSTHUMOUS AWARD

President Yar'Adua's recently decided to subject national award to critical reappraisal under the chairmanship of Justice Belgore. This vindicates Gani's rejection of the merit awards which are officially acknowledged to have been dispensed to criminals and politicised. VP Goodluck Jonathan's challenges to the Merit Award Committee are only meaningful if Yar'Adua's administration confers the highest post humous national award on the fallen hero and incorruptible patriot which Gani was.

INDUSTRY AND ENTERPRISE

Lastly Chief Gani will always be remembered for his remarkable enterprise, industry and knowledge economy. He fought against poverty not by begging for charity, hand outs but through productivity and wealth generation. The Bohemian rag tag comradeship was alien to Chief Gani Fawehimi. He was rich not through non performing loans but wealth generation through advocacy, litigation based on justice and fruits of his labour.

KNOWLEDGE INDUSTRY

His uninterrupted publication of law reports added value to the country's store of knowledge that tasks the creativity of our institutions of learning and intellectuals in general.

LIFE AFTER GANI

AFRICA NEEDS MORE OF KINDER COMPASSIONATE STRONGMEN AND WOMEN LIKE GANI

President Barrack Obama of USA advised in Ghana that "Africa doesn't need strongmen, it needs strong institutions." If strongmen are defined as Idi Amin, Mobutu Sese Seko and scores of Nigeria's wasteful dealers (not leaders!) yes, Africa does not need "strongmen". To that extent Obama was right. However if strongmen are seen as the Ganis, Mandelas, late Murtala Muhammed, Nkrumah, Aminu Kano, Ahmadu Bello, Chief Obafemi Awolowo, then Africa desperately needs more compassionate, courageous strongmen that must build sustainable institutions such that Gani left behind.

BLESSED IS THE DEAD

A South African writer noted that blessed are the dead for they shall not again be suspected. Gani will no more be suspected of perennial power failure, water shortages, non performing loans, closed universities, militancy in the Niger Delta, the widening gap between the poor and the rich and the pervasive underdevelopment of Nigeria amidst potential prosperity. The only way to mourn Gani is to fix Nigeria the way he desired. We the livings are the ones to be suspected of Nigeria's backwardness *not* Gani again!

GANI FOUGHT CANCER TO THE END

His physical body eventually succumbed to the scourge of cancer, but Gani spiritedly fought the disease as much as he fought corruption and bad governance. Report had it that as late as a fortnight ago, Gani sought visa to United States of America in his search for treatment. He first learnt that he had cancer three years ago. Nothing however changed Gani. In spite of the pains associated with cancer management, he exhibited same courage to the end with his active commentaries and prosecutions against injustice. What cancer could not do is to ebb his spirit. As a Muslim, Gani must have heeded the saying of the Holy Prophet that "if the last hour strikes and finds you carrying a sapling to the grove for planting, go ahead and plant it." Death is certainly inevitable, but Gani also taught us that it is our responses to death that matter.

May his grave be more spacious than the global space he positively and courageously impacted upon in the past 71 years of his eventful sojourn! May Almighty Allah shower the abundant blessings of this holy month of Ramadan on him, forgive his sins and console his dependants for the irreparable loss.

Justice Mustapha Akanbi: Private Citizen, Public Good*

"...almost everyone-regardless of income, available time, age, and skills-can do something useful for others and, in the process, strengthen the fabric of our shared a humanity"- Bill Clinton-*Giving* (2007)

All roads (sorry, all committed minds that nowadays ply the Nigeria's miserable roads) lead to Ilorin, Kwara state this Thursday, 5th of November for the formal commissioning of the three-year old Justice Akanbi Foundation (MAF) as well as the turbanning of its founder as the *Wakilin* of Ilorin. Precisely because yours truly has been somehow privileged to be counted and *involved* (apology to Chief Emeka Ojukwu) with this great humanitarian process, I bear testimony that Mustapha Akanbi Foundation (*MAF*) is coming of age in the art of giving in a country of official non-giving, official grabbing, elite greed and state denials of roads, light, water and security of lives and property. Inaugurated in Ilorin, Kwara State on the 12th of September 2006, MAF is adding value in this notorious age of national value-subtractions. Out of simple and enduring noble objective to serve as "…a veritable platform for promoting democratic values and fostering sustainable and viable democratic development in Nigeria," MAF, within the past activist three years, has left bold imprints in areas of Education, Human empowerment, health, Anti-corruption campaign and good governance. The foundation is also expected to carry out planning, research and

* *Daily Trust* (Monday, November 2, 2009)

review in areas of interest consistent with the foundation's goal; to monitor and evaluate both public and private programmes and practices in business concerns and transactions; and to be in vanguard of promoting the full realization of man's potential through wholesome education, creative works, capacity building and productive skills acquisition. Apart from significant humanitarian work which has raised hope for the sick and disabled, the Foundation is *catching them young* via reading and writing skill acquisitions in public secondary schools.

The Foundation *is acting local but thinking global* through high profile public agenda setting lectures. The chairman of the Foundation and former Chairman of Independent Corrupt Practices Commission (ICPC), Honourable Justice Mustapha Akanbi has commendably come out with sustainable initiative to further continue in retirement same good work spanning some decades at the bar and the bench. Justice Akanbi has served both as a state and non-state actor and very well too. Early this year, MAF organised a one day work shop on the "Causes of Diabetes, Management and Control". In 2008, the Foundation conducted a free training workshop on Tie & Dye for some selected creative individuals. The Foundation has visited and made donations to the various institutions. It organizes pilot scheme on reading and writing of English language for junior secondary school students

The singular commitment, passion and courage of Justice Akanbi manifest in yearly topical themes that elevate public debate from the pedestrian. MAF, organised a symposium on 'Participatory Democracy and Good Governance as Fundamental Tools Sustainable Development in 2006'. The first anniversary Public lecture held in February last year at Ladi Kwali held at Sheraton Hotel, Abuja on the theme "*Participatory Democracy and Good Governance*".

The lecture entitled the "*Challenges of Nations Building: The Case of Nigeria*" was ably delivered by Professor Ibrahim Agboola Gambari, Under-Secretary-general and special adviser to the UN Secretary-General. Therein Professor Gambari commendably brought to the fore, the increasingly endangered notions of nation-hood and nation-building. No country has uncritically embraced the myth of globalization than Nigeria. On the one hand, Nigeria's master-leaders (or are they servant-leaders?) had demonstrated more confidence in "foreign investment" rather than unbundling the latent huge domestic energy for growth and development. Former President Olusegun Obasanjo uncritically spent more time ostensibly wooing investors than concentrating on cultivating and building critical institutions of the nation that would make investment, (foreign or local) to thrive. Since then the nation has been imperilled with collapsed domestic investment and institutional decay. On the other hand, there are citizens who carry on as if it does not matter if their country exists or not. Professor Gambari reminded the latter, no less than the former that today, there are millions of stateless citizens in the world on account of failed states and collapsed nations stressing the need for Nigerians to renew commitment to nation-building given that the alternatives are simply unthinkable. What professor Gambari however diplomatically ignored was the painful truism that many Nigerians were and still are voluntarily giving up their citizenship for that of other countries, no thanks to failing Nigerian state service delivery. Chinua Achebe is officially counted in the United States of America (USA) as African American making the point that a nation is not just a group of people but well-living and secured people. Nobody can fault Professor Gambari's shared perspective that in this so-called Global village, we must still be conscious of our respective clans as well as the respective challenges that go with that. The hope is that this year's anniversary Lecture would offer another menu of ideas for national and global discourse. The topic of this year's lecture is *Democratic Governance and Political leadership in Africa* to be delivered by Professor Akintunde Oshuntokun. Coming barely a month from MO Ibrahim leadership Award searched in vain for an African leader recipient, it will be spiritually uplifting to hear how the continent can reinvent leadership.

Rimi: In Praise of Audacity[*]

"Fighters never say goodbye" - *Gracia Machel*

Somehow, Barrack Obama, (now President of United States of America, USA) popularizes the politics of audacity (of hope). The late Abubakar Rimi, the former Kano State Governor (who died due to complications arising from the Easter break robbery tragedy) however must truly be credited with the original audacious democratic politics of the twenty-first century. Rimi must be politically audacious to have opted for Northern Elements Progressive Union (NEPU) and not Northern People Congress, (NPC) to kick-start a five decade long activist eventful political carrier. NEPU promoted unapologetic open politics of resistance. By joining NEPU with the attendant repression of its members by the combined forces of traditional rulership and conservative NPC, Rimi must have known that his political road was destined to be rough. Many politicians would have opted for least resistance political road anyway. Today we daily witness unprincipled lot who from the political entry point opt for "winning" parties, (not winning principles). During the second Republic, PRP was a diametrical political ideological contrast to NPN. Of course there were three other political parties in between, namely, Unity Party of Nigeria, (UPN), Great Nigeria Peoples Party, (GNPP), and Nigerian People Party, (NPP). Asserting his right to be different, Abubakar Rimi together with his political mentor, late Aminu Kano and other colleagues converged in Kaduna to proclaim the PRP. The choice of

* *Daily Trust*, 12th April 2010

Kaduna on October 21st 1978 for the proclamation of PRP was in itself audacious and historically exceptional. Other parties held their inaugural conventions in Lagos, the then nation's capital. PRP announced democratic socialism as its ideology: "an ideology which teaches self reliance and the takeover of our economy from the grip of neo-colonialists into the hands of the people." The party in power through its actions and programmes made the historic point: a party does not have to taunt territorial spread (think of the so-called largest party in Africa!) before it offers qualitative representation and articulation. It controlled two old states, namely Kano (now Kano and Jigawa states) and Kaduna (present Kaduna and Katsina states) in the then Federation of 19 states. But the real opposition to NPN in terms of radical alternative audacious politics of change during the second Republic was PRP. PRP abolished the notorious hated *haraji (head tax), jangali and ushira* taxes with public mass applause. The party set national agenda for the ruling "largest" NPN to follow. Governor Rimi of Kano State and Balarabe Musa of Kaduna state were the first democratically elected governors to audaciously declare May Day a public holiday in 1980. The ruling NPN federal government followed in the progressive trail of the PRP in 1981. Thanks to the dynamic competitive political environment of that era. Another Rimi's political landmark that readily comes to mind in this age of easy memory loss was the second triennial delegates' conference of NLC which held in 1981. The NPN administration's preference was a subservient Chief David Ojeli of the Civil Service Union as NLC president as distinct from the radical Hassan Sunmonu. Alhaji Hassan Sunmonu was eventually re-elected second term President of the Congress in an historic conference hosted by Rimi administration in Kano at the then prestigious Central Hotel. The courageous and progressive Rimi government offered a free atmosphere for the country's labour movement to hold the conference unfettered in which votes truly counted. Audacious Rimi set up the first state City Television to break the top-down monopoly news (read: propaganda) of the NTA. Audacious Rimi set up the first state newspaper, Triumph (and Abishir) newspapers which for once challenged the then federal newspapers, namely *New Nigeria* and *Daily Times* in terms of battle of ideas and even coverage.

I started my working carrier as a journalist with *Triumph* newspapers. As a privileged pioneer staff of *Triumph* newspaper, I bear witness that the late Abubakar Rimi had the audacity of tolerance. I, together with scores of us, my editor, Ibrahim Rufai, late Abdurrahman Black, Muhammed Lawal, Sunny Iyang were certainly not PRP card-carrying members. On the contrary, we were *left of the* PRP (in fact, some us were to the *left of the left of PRP*!). Triumph Company operated in government House before it built its permanent office. Yet we were freely tolerated as reporters in government house. Dr Haroun Adamu-led management of the progressive state newspaper (*Triumph*) allowed us to report as we saw it. Many times, we were even encouraged to be critical of the PRP policies and programmes. When PRP was factionalized, the two factions (*santsi and topo*) had free expressions in the public platform that was independent Triumph newspapers. *The point can therefore not be overstated: audacious Rimi served as a governor in developmentalist Nigeria. The real issue then was urgent and rapid development of Nigeria. Governance was about common wealth, not personal accumulation.* It was the age of idealism in which a governor was just one among equals, not the present day Nigeria in which most governors and their cronies behave like *King Kongs* bulling their way through rather than convincing their followers. Rimi's method was unapologetically civil and civilian throughout. Without a troop or battalion, we all witness the hundreds of thousands who audaciously came to bury him. He controversially served Abacha as a Minister of Communication. But, it was not surprising that he clashed with the dictatorship and was even jailed by Abacha for audaciously insisting on good governance and return to democracy. His testimony at the *Kangaroo* military tribunal of Buhari/Idi Agbon on so-called assets recovery was a testimony in the art of courage to say NO to politically motivated trial.

Of course, Rimi fell for political opportunism. This later diminished his consistent progressive credentials. But even in political opportunism, Rimi audaciously asserted his right to be radically different nonetheless. He and others were expelled from PRP for having the audacity to challenge the leadership of the late Mallam Aminu Kano. But Rimi was counted on the political *left* of the dominant PRP. He had the late Michael Imoudu, the militant veteran labour leader as the factional leader of his faction. Many Rimi's admirers including yours sincerely were least impressed to see Rimi as visible actor in PDP during the current dispensation especially with strange ideological bedfellows. But we were not surprised that even in PDP, Rimi audaciously stood against the dominant forces of establishment in PDP insisting on level playing field and transparency. PDP must eventually come to value internal party democracy, (for now the party democracy's internal is dead!). if it does so, the party is eternally indebted to Rimi who audaciously (in tradition of radical contestations of NEPU and PRP) broke ranks with the party bureaucracy to contest against Obasanjo in 1999 and 2003. *Nigeria has never produced a civilian politician who courageously stood against militicians in Nigeria's politics like late Abubakar Rimi.*

Nobody bargains for cheap and callous death arising from terrorism inflicted by road marauders. The tragic death of a 70 year old ruling People's Democratic Party (PDP) chieftain is a wake-up tragic call that lives are endangered in Nigeria.

In the 1980s when Alhaji Rimi Abubakar was the governor of Kano State, Nigeria was safe such that travelling at 10pm was a pleasure not tears and sorrow of today. May Allah make his grave spacious for comfort.

Yar'Adua in Praise of Civility*

THE DEATH

With great sorrow and deep sense of loss we received the news of the departure of the President and Commander and Chief of the Federal Republic of Nigeria, Alhaji Umaru Musa Yar'Adua GCFR who died at the late hours of Wednesday May 5, 2010 after a protracted illness.

INDUSTRY-SUPPORTIVE

The late President Yar'Adua showed appreciable unprecedented commitment and determination to re-industrialise and re-electrify Nigeria.

His administration raised the prospects of industrialisation and wealth generation in the country more than ever before. He delineated wealth generation vision for the Federal Republic of Nigeria in his inaugural address of May 29 2007 whem he promised at the level of the economy to do "*necessary work to create more jobs, lower interest rates, reduce inflation and maintain a stable exchange rate.*"

President Yar'Adua rekindled hope in industrialisation and reaffirmed his belief in the primacy of industrial renaissance as indisputable factor in poverty eradication. The late President Yar'Adua singled out the textile industry as the "*largest manufacturing in this country that must be protected.*" For once, he transformed policy rhetoric of the past administration with respect to textile intervention fund to policy reality through disbursement of revival fund via the Bank of Industry. We also witnessed an activist Presidency through the former Minister of Finance, Dr. Mansur Muktar and his

---

* *Daily Trust* 5th June 2010

Economic Adviser, Tanimu Yakubu, taking stock of the existing collapsed industries and partnering with Kaduna state government in particular to revive the textile industries. Of course, the industries have not been revived; the late Yar'Adua's concern and sensitivity had prevented total collapse altogether.

The challenge is for the newly sworn in President Jonathan to realise the vision of reindustrialization of the country, create mass jobs and put an end to the existing intolerable poverty in the land.

LABOUR-FRIENDLY

Perhaps no President of Nigeria has demonstrated enough cooperation AND engagement with organised labour like the late President Yar'Adua. He strongly believed in constructive dialogue and not war of industrial attrition of OBJ era. President Yar'Adua demonstrated great commitment to address critical issues affecting labour including the minimum wage. He set up the Presidential Committee on new minimum wage headed by retired Justice Babatunde Alfa Belgore, whose committee just concluded its work. He kept faith with agreement with labour on the issue of petrol pricing since 2007. His administration has not increased the price of products and never incresead VAT as agreed with labour. When compared with serial price increases under OBJ, we would appreciate that Nigeria has lost a sensitive leader. On the contrary, President Yar'Adua actually reduced the product price to N65 in line with the global trends of downward fall in international price of crude oil. Of course we witnessed prolong ASUU/NASU/SSANU strikes under him, but it was to the eternal credit of Yar'Adua that he never criminalize industrial relations as was the norms during the past discredited military/quasi-military dispensations.

GOOD GOVERNANCE

By and large the late President's attitude to governance was commendable. He espoused and promoted soft issues in governance: civility, accountability and transparency in public service. He historically peacefully resolved the crisis in Niger-Delta through the amnesty programme of arms for freedom. Today, oil production in the country has gone up due to the relative peace in the Niger Delta.

His insistence in the rule of law ensured the emergency of governors like Peter Obi in Anambra State, Adams Oshiomhole in Edo State and Olusegun Mimiko in Ondo State even when the governors are not from his political party. The late President was the first to acknowledge that the election that brought him to power was flawed. He went further to set up the electoral reform Committee headed by Justice Uwais. He never interfered with the judicial process or oversight function of the National Assembly.

THE DEAD WOULD NOT BE SUSPECTED

The burden is on all of us who are living to ensure we maintain and improve the profound legacy he left behind We particularly call on President Goodluck Jonathan to maintain the best governance practices of Yar'Adua.

On behalf of the National Executive Council of the Union and the generality of our members, we sympathize with the family of the late President in particular, his wife, Hajia Turai Yar'Adua, his mother, the newly sworn in President and Commander-in-Chief, Dr. Goodluck Jonathan, the government and people of Katsina State and the entire country for this great loss.

May the gentle soul of our departed President Yar'Adua rest in Allah's bossom.

Yar'Adua: Farewell to Civility*

Since the late Prime Minister, Tafawa Balewa and Alhaji Shehu Shagari, the late President Umaru Musa Yar'Adua would be credited with a return of civility to federal governance. His death must not mark the end of civility in governance. Better positively put; let us uphold Yar'Adua's legacy by demanding and insisting on civil conduct on the part of public affairs managers. Not few Presidents (including one military prototype) had acted philosopher-kings interpreting Nigerian reality with boring words, (spoken but not meant). For Yar'Adua, it seemed it was time to change the country for the better rather than sermonizing. His inaugural address on May 29th 2007 was refreshingly brief. Readers/listeners alike were spared the burden of information overload often associated with Presidential speeches in this country. It was all bagfuls of *minimum presidential words and maximum presidential policy initiatives, if you like.* The brevity of Yar'Adua's speeches did not diminish the essence of his messages. On the contrary, one major significant feature of his inaugural speech was memory. Huge historical deficits were the norms in presidential addresses. There was hardly any reference to the positive landmarks of the past. OBJ defined Nigeria only (and only) in reference to his first military tenure and second civilian coming which were ever presented as the "glorious" moments for Nigeria. With remarkable difference, Yar'Adua rightly drew on country's huge historic heritage. He urged Nigerians to "capture the mood of optimism that defined us at the dawn of independence..." Refreshingly for once, he acknowledged his predecessor's efforts. Despite wholesome violence, deaths and acrimonies, being regular trademarks of his predecessor's

* *Daily Trust*, 9th May 2010

regime, late President Yar'Adua had an eye on the bigger pictures as distinct from the black spots. He simply moved on in civility to observe the emerging trends in the past eight years, namely national consensus on deepening democracy, rule of law, market economy, anti-corruption campaign and good governance. He pledged his commitment to all the issues. The real acid test for the new government was the last minute arbitrary oil product price increases and 100 per cent in VAT. After the strike led by Nigeria Labour Congress (NLC), Yar'Adua negotiated with organized labour. To his eternal credit, until his death, he upheld the spirit and content of that singular agreement not to further increase the products price without consultation with stakeholders. Indeed, Yar'Adua did the unprecedented: did not increase products' price at all but rather reduced the price from 70 to 65 naira per litre. The dividend of Yar'Adua's civility for the nation was relative industrial peace since 2007. In three years Obasanjo administration arbitrarily marked up prices almost four times, with attendant national strikes. Conversely Yar'Adua's administration did not record a single national strike. Only President Shehu Shagari's administration dared to parallel Yar'Adua's record in industrial harmony. The former witnessed only two-day national strike in 1981 over the demand of Hassan Sunmonu-led NLC for new minimum wage. Immediate reversal of this policy suicide of price increases in the twilight of Obasanjo administration showed we were set for a new dispensation of sensitivity in governance. It institutionalized social dialogue as distinct from criminalization as means of engagement with labour.

Yar'Adua elected to be a "*servant leader*" who will be a "*listener*" and "*doer*" and "*serve with humility*". It is left for historians to assess if he actually led as a servant leader. But what cannot be disputed is the fact that President Musa Umar Yar'Adua was the first to consciously dare to declare the leadership type. Past leaders simply led either for the better (more in deficit) or for the worse (more in surplus) after which the citizens came to terms with their leadership styles.

Precious things come in small packages", so goes the popular marketing wisdom. Just by a stroke of presidential gesture and surprise, late President Yar'Adua made public his declared assets to the Code of Conduct Bureau. By doing so, he qualitatively elevated the anti-corruption discourse more than the pedestrian and the symbolic disaster/public relations mess of the past. In terms of its surprise content and its radical presentation, the President's Assets Declaration form was only paralleled in history by General Murtala Muhammad's surprise and dazzling leadership-by-example of the 1970s.

Whatever his net worth, we had for once in public domain the detail- figures of his cash-at-hands, bank balances and loans and even the material profile of his wife. It was a radical probity and accountability Renaissance of a kind. The impact assessment of Yar'Adua's public Assets declaration was far-reaching.

Hitherto, anti-corruption campaign had gathered dust and had even been completely undermined by perception of selectivity, partial disclosures, plain persecution, *other-ness* as distinct from *all-ness,* victimization and even blatant partisanship. *By a singular force of example, late President Yar'Adua shifted the partial dim probity searchlight from some few others to a full blown beam on all public holders including him. My investigation shows that the late President, (three years after presiding over the Federation) has no single house in Abuja.* Yar'Adua's disinterestedness in the pervasive elitist self-having and his commitment to commonwealth was a worthy extra-ordinary imprudence to the criminal legacies of scores of Abuja's land-grabbers, who not only allocated to themselves, but their spouses and children. He was a stalwart advocate of rule of law. The reversal of the twin policies of VAT and fuel prices increases was done on the ground that OBJ government jumped due process in the policy pronouncement. Supreme Court pronouncement with respect to Anambra state was promptly enforced making governor Peter Obi the first executive beneficiary of the rule of law in the new dispensation. Lagos state federation money was refunded following a correct interpretation of the Supreme Court judgment. The reversal of the sale of refineries was also done on account of undue bidding and processes. While the antagonists and protagonists of Soludo's Naira agenda were at loggerheads it took the eagle eye of the Anthony General of the Federation to realise that Soludo jumped the CBN Act to grandstand. Never before has a government recorded such qualitative achievements by singular stroke of quality policy control measure with respect to application of the rule of law. For a nation used to hard drivers, not few did the growling and snarling at the perceived go-slow of Yar'Adua. But at the last count, we now know that what the nation needs desperately are soft leadership issues, namely integrity, peace, dialogue and engagement. On Niger Delta, Yar'Adua exposed the madness of war as a tool of official engagement with aggrieved citizens. In return we are all better for it with improved oil production in the region and restored hope for development. *President Jonathan Goodluck must prove that it not yet the end of history to civility in governance with the death of President Yar'Adua.* Let us be ruled by knowledge and brains not some raw brawls. The real acid test for continuous civility as practiced by the late President is that our votes must count next year. May Allah make his grave peaceful for eternal comfort.

Mandela: Age and Ideas*

Last year, 2009, the United Nations (UN) declared 18th of July every year as Nelson Mandela Day. He was 92 years old yesterday. Mandela is the only living genuine icon and former Head of State to be so honoured by the global body, i.e. United Nations (UN), made up of 192 countries. When we add non-members like the Vatican City and Kosovo who all celebrate Mandela, we know that we truly marked the birthday of No. 1 global citizen yesterday. UN agreed to commemorate Mandela's birthday every year to recognise the "Nobel Peace Prize laureate's contribution to resolving conflicts and promoting race relations, human rights and reconciliation."

Mandela's story is never boring for all Africans seeking for a better continent and indeed a better world. His birthday name was Rolihlahla which in Xhosa language means "*pulling the branch of a tree*" and according to Nelson Mandela himself, means "trouble maker". We somehow live up to our name. His father's name was Gadla Henry Mphakanyiswa. Mandela's father was a traditional chief by blood and custom. Indeed Nelson Mandela was being groomed to become a chief. As a sign of respect, he is called Madiba, named after his Madiba clan. Fate and the compelling oppressive reality of his country, South Africa made him to join and eventually lead the struggle against Apartheid in South Africa. Apartheid was a racist system of government. White minority brutally imposed its discriminatory and oppressive rule against the majority black people. Mandela truly lived up to his birthday name. He became truly a trouble maker to the racist regime. Apartheid lasted for 30 years (1948-1978). For as long as Apartheid lasted Mandela and his other comrades fought the oppressive regime. In 1964 Mandela and others

* *Daily Trust*, 19th July 2010

that included Walter Sisulu, Govan Mbeki, and Raymond were all sentenced to life imprisonment. He spent 27 years on the notorious Robben Island prison.

This year also marks 20th anniversary of his release from prison following worldwide campaign led by countries that included Nigeria. Paradoxically most European governments, notably that of Britain, and America supported the racist regime and incarceration of Nelson Mandela whom they labelled ""“terrorist”. Mandela's auto-biography, *Long Walk to Freedom* (1994), is a compulsory read for all Africans willing to appreciate the power of resistance and sacrifice. What lessons for Mandela's life? Who leads like him in Nigeria?

Mandela's deserved freedom, proves that time is longer than the Apartheid rope. Mandela is credited with scores of leadership virtues. They include courage, principle, sacrifice, forgiveness, love and reconciliation and non- vengeance among others. *The way Mandela generously forgives and reconciles with his white racist tormentors shows that we can forgive and move on even if we do not forget.*

Another singular leadership quality of Madiba, (the “old man”) is “making oneself dispensable”, i.e. dispensability of leaders. In a continent reputed for sit tight leaders (Egypt's Mubarak, Zimbabwe's Mugabe, Libya's Gaddafi, late Bongo of Gabon and President Muzeveni of Uganda) Mandela shows that it is not how long power is exercised but how it is creatively humanly used to uplift peoples and societies. His one term five-year tenure (1994-1999) as the President of a non-racial, democratic Republic offers lessons in leadership for Federal Republic of Nigeria. Given the current crisis of leadership, Nigeria's leaders must emulate Mandela's model of representation and delegation and even resignation. In 1996, two years he assumed power, Nelson Mandela said that: “*I must step down when there are one or two people who admire me.*” Nigeria's leaders must accept the reality of exit once they assume power. The protagonists/antagonists of 2011 agenda must reflect on the Mandela's spirit.

Former President Olusegun Obasanjo refused Mandela formula. Today he is permanently discredited as a sit-tight greedy/power mongering leader, while Mandela is credited with modesty in exercise of power.

Paradoxically Nigeria among other countries fought for the liberation of South Africa. Leadership lessons expectedly should rather flow from Nigeria not from South Africa. Two years before he left office in 1999, Nelson Mandela stopped chairing cabinet meetings. His then Vice-President, Thabo Mbeki was reportedly in charge. He had a good rapport with Vice-President Mbeki such that he was reported at different forums celebrating him (Mbeki) as a better administrator than himself. He indeed modestly attributed many great ideas he championed to his Vice-President, Tambo Mbeki. Our leaders should learn the virtues of comradeship from Mandela. Governors who engage their deputies in wars of attrition are not acting in the spirit of Mandela.

His presidency was inaugurated in 1994. He took pride in the knowledge that ANC boasts of scores of leaders that can rule South Africa. Madiba related cordially even with his political rivals. During his historic presidency, Mandela even allowed his arch rival and die hard apologist of Apartheid regime, Mr Mangosutu Buthelezi as Acting President while he was on overseas trips that also involved his Vice President, Thabo Mbeki. He is a living voice for Africa and the world.

President George W Bush and Vice- President Dick Cheney of America criminally invaded Iraq in 2002. Nelson Mandela's comment on the war was as resonant as the invaders' bombs. According to Mandela, Bush administration's advisers were like "dinosaurs" who did not want President Bush to "*belong to the modern age*" adding that US was a threat to world peace given its penchant for impunity and unilateralism. The eventual withdrawal of US troops from Iraq vindicates Mandela's timely moral intervention. Africa is indebted to Mandela for his campaign for 2010 hosting right of FIFA soccer tournament on the continent.

Most elders are conservative and shy to talk about HIV/AIDS. Nelson Mandela was the first to openly disclose that he lost his son to HIV/AIDS and called for an open fight against the scourge. He combines old age with refreshingly new modern ideas. He is a lover of sports (soccer) at 92. Nigeria's leaders should emulate Nelson Mandela, think global and act local. *It is a shame that national leaders are endangered species in Nigeria while regional leaders have taken over the country.*

We read of Northern/Southern leaders. Where are Nigerian leaders? Where are Pan-African leaders like Mandela?

Hassan Sunmonu (At 70) For Beginners*

Comrade Alhaji Hassan Adebayo (HA) Sunmonu OON, Secretary-General, Organization of African Trade Union Unity (OATUU) based in Accra will be 70 years old today on Friday, 7th of January 2011. The pioneer founding President of Nigeria Labour Congress (NLC) and twice elected NLC President (1978 to 1984) was born with his twin identical brother, Engr Hussein Sunmonu (the difference not clear at all!) on 7th January, 1941 at Oshogbo, in Osun State. What has time got to do with the birth of heroes, great men and women alike? The old received wisdom has it that; *there is time and place for everything.* Indeed everything is said to be good in its season. 1940s was a watershed in the history of colonial Nigeria. Nazi Germany led by Adolf Hitler was suffocating the world in imperial war of attrition which in turn led to the historic Allied resistance against fascism. British colonialists, (as part of the allied forces), enlisted the colonialized natives from India to Nigeria, Burma to Ghana for the war priorities at the expense of social welfare. True to its exploitative character, British colonialism shifted the burden of the war efforts on the colonialized natives. It stepped up direct taxation, massive retrenchment of workers in the nascent public sectors, casualisation of the workforce and arbitrarily ordered recalculation of monthly pay to hourly rates. In Nigeria just as well as in other colonies, these exploitative measures radicalized the nascent trade unions, principally the Union of Railwaymen. From their relative hitherto moderate engagement with colonial authority on employment issues via petition-writings, they moved to direct confrontation with colonial authority. Tasking the imagination of

* January 7, 2011 (*Guardian*)

historians, interestingly the same 1941, the very year HA was born was the same year Michael Imoudu was incensed by the arrogance of Colonial railways employers and he later became Labour Number 1 and a kind of *bête noire* of colonial government. Imoudu in 1941 led hundreds of railway workers in spontaneous peaceful protest from Ebute Metta to Government House in Lagos Island, a distance of some eight kilometres to register their protest to the then colonial governor, Sir Bernerd Bourdillion against arbitrary lock-out of the railway workers and poor working conditions in general. With this singular direct mass action by railway workers, and subsequent strikes of the 1940s, Nigeria's trade union grew in strength from house unions to national Federations leading to the formation of Trade Union Congress (TUC) in 1943. Significantly too, the time Alhaji Hassan Adebayo (HA) Sunmonu was born was the same decade of heightened nationalism. In the 1940s, early nationalists, namely Azikwe and Awolowo through their combative progressive journalism had spotlighted the demands of the workers and linked the workers' protest to the need for total independence and an end to colonial domination. This historic context perhaps explains why today HA at 70 is an acknowledged tested, committed trade unionist, a patriot, a pan African and a global citizen of profound integrity. Mentored in a regional developmentalist Nigeria HA is a product of the then functional public schools. He started his education career at Ansar-Ud-Deen School in Oshogbo between 1948 and 1950 and All Saints School, Oshogbo between 1950 and 1954, where he got his First School Leaving Certificate in December 1954. In 1955, he went to Oshogbo Grammar School where he stayed for about 14 months before he moved to Yaba Technical Institute in September, 1957. He obtained his General Certificate in Education (GCE) Ordinary Level in 1961. He later bagged the Secondary Technical Certificate, moved to Yaba College of Technology between 1961 to 1964 where he obtained the Ordinary National Diploma (OND) in Civil Engineering, the Higher National Diploma (HND) in Civil Engineering. HA proceeded to Italy for a Post-Graduate Diploma Course in Highway Engineering.

Born against the historic resistance against workplace oppression and struggle for independence, HA was almost an activist by birth.

Comrade Hassan Sunmonu was once an active Students' Union leader; Secretary, Muslim Students' Society (MSS) Yaba Technical Institute Branch between 1958 and 1961, National Auditor, Muslim Students' Union Society of Nigeria between 1962 and 1967, the President, Yaba College of Technology Students' Union between September 1966 and June, 1967. He was the President, National Association of Technological Students (NATS) between September 1966 and June, 1967 and Second Vice President, National Union of Nigerian Students (NUNS) between September 1966 and June 1967. It was inevitable and logical that he would become spokesman for the working people through trade union representation at workplace. His trade union carrier with his integrity intact has spanned well over 4 decades! He was once the 2nd Assistant Secretary (International), Public Works Aerodrome Technical and General Works' Union of Nigeria between August 1974 and November 1977; President, Civil Service Technical Workers Union of Nigeria between November, 1977 and February, 1981; President, Nigeria Labour Congress between February 1978 and February, 1984; Director of Industrial Relations, Civil Service Technical Workers Union of Nigeria between March 1984 and October, 1986. HA is currently the Secretary-General, Organisation of African Trade Union Unity (OATUU) from October 1986 to date. He is also Deputy Presiding Officer, Economic, Social and Cultural Council (ECOSOCC) of the African Union, since September 2008 to date. HA belongs to the second generation of unionists in Nigeria and indeed in Africa. Following the recommendations of the notorious Justice Adebiyi Tribunal of Inquiry into the Activities of the Trade Unions in 1977, some unionists including Chief Michael Imoudu were banned from trade union activities. Under the controversial policy of "guided democracy" and "limited government intervention", the military regime of Obasanjo had aimed at cultivating a tamed and subservient labour centre. However the workers reaffirmed their preference for independent organization by electing Hassan Sunmonu as the first President of the restructured Congress in 1978 with others like Mr D.C. Ojeli, Mr P.O. Ero-Philips, late M. E. Mpamugo, Deputy President, treasurer and deputy treasurer respectively. HA's leadership of NLC from 1978 to 1984 is a compulsory read for today's trade unionists on how to operate under a new democratic dispensation. NLC under HA fought and won the battle to make May 1st a public holiday, fought and won the struggle for a new minimum wage of N125 ($240) in 1981 after a successful nation-wide strike under President Shehu Shagari's administration. Notwithstanding the divisive strategy of the second Republic politicians aimed at splitting the NLC, into "democrats" and "Marxists" HA sustained the unity of the trade movement through all inclusive ideologically driven movement. This was consolidated upon by his successor, Alhaji Ali Chiroma until 1988 when Babangida regime militarily dissolved the NLC's executive Council. Very few unionists talked straight to power like Hassan Sunmonu does as a labour leader. The historic Charter of Demands under HA leadership remains the first agenda setting document for decent work by the Nigeria's working class. HA led NLC to build the first historic formal alliance between trade unions and the university academics and students. Yours sincerely was a direct beneficiary of working class solidarity under HA. After Ango Abdullahi's dictatorship in ABU expelled us twilight of graduation, through the instrumentality of Committee of Vice Chancellors we were further denied our transcripts, preventing us from moving into other universities. HA in alliance with ASUU led by late Dr Modibo of ABU intervened for transcripts release that made us complete our first degrees. As a worker Comrade Hassan Sunmonu had added value to developmentalist Nigeria. As an engineer with Federal Ministry of works, he worked on so many offices and roads project that included Zaria–Kano Road Reconstruction; Igolo –Porto Novo Road (Benin Republic); Dualization of Denton Causeway (Oyingbo – Iddo, Lagos) by direct labour; Construction of the National Arts Theatre, Lagos; and Construction of the Third Mainland Bridge, Lagos, among others. Married with six adult children, a devout Muslim HA is one of the few intellectual activist global unionists standing today. A multi-linguist; he is fluent in Yoruba, (with bagful of proverbs!) fluent in English, French, Italian and Twi (Ghanaian language). HA has been honoured nationally and internationally. Recipient of Officer of the Order of the Niger (OON) on 18th December, 2001, he was also honoured with the National order of Burkina Faso in December,

2009. Happy 70th birthday to both Alhajis Hassan and Hussein Sunmonu!!

Keeping Fit at Fifty*

"*At 50, everyone has the face he deserves*" once observed by George Owen! Paradoxically Owen died before 50. He lived from year 1903 to year 1950. Yet, at some forty seven odd years, George Owen deservedly had an undisputable face of a British journalist and a renowned global author of the most famous novels of the 20th century, namely '*Animal Farm*' and '*Nineteen Eighty-Four*'. Jesus Christ, Prophet Isa (Peace be upon him) died at 30, yet his prophet hood was crystal clear as that of one of the oldest of the prophets; Prophet Nuhu (peace be on him). Prophet Muhammed (Peace on him) received prophesy at 40! General Yakubu Gowon presided over Federal Nigeria at the tender age of 30. Indeed General Gowon married while in office. Yet he successfully managed an unfortunate civil war, presided over an unprecedented national reconciliation known in history. At forty seven, Barack Obama deservedly puts a "black" face on a seat of imperial power so-named; *White House* (so called obviously certainly not with an African occupant in mind!) What then has age got to do about who we are? At 92 Nelson Mandela remains a living moral authority with such global outreach that many a canonized saint hardly covered. Listening to any of the ever green Reggae lyrics of the late Bob Marley who packed up at the tender age of 35, it is just as if Bob Marley is with us. *If we judge in terms of what we hold dearly and what we passionately belief in, professionally it can be said that nobody ultimately has an age after-all.* Prophets are not followed because of their age but because of their messages of redemptions. Many remember that Fidel Castro led the great Cuban revolution that sacked once and for all the US backed Batista dictatorship. But few

* 17th January 2011

recall that Fidel Castro was just 32 years old. Looking at the mirror, when I clocked 50 a week ago, yours sincerely still wonders if my face says it all. Nonetheless thank God that a child of independent Nigeria remains standing no less than the country is. Marking the golden anniversary, yours truly was inspired by the old received wisdom that "the secret of longevity is to stay breathing". For almost a decade now I have come to appreciate the health benefits of keeping fit through regular exercise. For the greatest overall health benefits, experts recommend that you do 20 to 30 minutes of aerobic activity three or more times a week and some type of muscle strengthening activity and stretching out at least twice a week. Regular exercise reduces the risk of dying prematurely, reduces the risk of dying prematurely from heart disease, reduces the risk of developing diabetes and reduces the risk of developing high blood pressure among others. Many thanks, to scores of friends and comrades who at the shortest notice planned the walkout and came out on a windy cold Saturday to do a two hour fitness walk in marking my birthday under the theme; *keeping fit for a better Nigeria and Greater Africa.* What ordinarily passes for personal indulgence turned to be mass fun for a multitude at Murtala Square in Kaduna. Many thanks to Alhaji Balarabe Musa, first Executive governor of Kaduna state who at 75 inspired all and completed the two hour walk out. Not surprising that a week after he audaciously picked the PRP ticket as gubernatorial candidate. If fitness translates to votes and vote counts, I bear witness that Alhaji Balarabe Musa can return to Sir Kashim Ibrahim House in May this year. Special thanks to Kaduna state commissioner for Youths and Sports, Honourable Abdulazeez Mohammed who, representing Governor Patrick Yakowa demystified governance and joined to keep fit in a classless movement. Many past and serving world leaders are known to work out regularly while in office. Nelson Mandela singled out keeping fit in prison as one antidote against the restrictive humiliation of Apartheid regime. Bill Clinton is known for jogging, George W. Bush for biking, (not just bombing!) and George H.W. Bush for golfing. America's newest First Family reportedly takes fitness to a whole new level. Both President Barack Obama and First Lady Michelle Obama are early-morning regulars at the gym, and their daughters Malia and Sasha play sports at school. "The First

Grandma, Marian Robinson, returned to her teen-age pursuit of track and field in her fifties and sixties. Even during the gruelling, two-year campaign, then-candidate Obama reportedly kept up his workouts. He would rise early in the morning to hit the nearest gym in whatever city he happened to be visiting." His typical workout is 45 minutes long. *It will be refreshingly uplifting seeing the pictures of our serving governors and President alike regardless of party affiliations, regularly walking out in fitness exercise with their fellow citizens. They don't need to meet citizens only when elections are around the corner.* Besides the walkout for my birthday, my best birthday gift is encapsulated in the serial primaries of political parties. As a child of democratic independent Nigeria, am excited to be 50 not under military dictatorship. Regardless of its imperfections, democratic Nigeria is preferred to jackboot regimes which once suffocated the country for the worse. INEC must be commended for ordering the party primaries which have brought out the good, the bad and even the worse aspects of our political parties in particular and the democratic process in general. But democratic process nonetheless! Only democratic process would expose the hypocrisy of affirmative action on women participation in politics. *Witness how female delegates at the PDP spread their votes among two men, Goodluck Jonathan and Abubakar Atiku and ignored the only female aspirant, Sarah Jibril. So much for gender and first lady's women initiative!* Only democracy would bring to the fore elegantly the limit of political nepotism. Witness Kwara state where Saraki family is at political war in which anything but harmony is possible. Blood might be thicker than water. But in a democratic process, it is not about which one is thicker. On the contrary, the blood and the water are desirable in proper mix for survival. Witness how some governors in the North legitimately expose the myth of regionalism and opted for self preservation during the PDP presidential primary. Even those reportedly said to vote for Atiku did so out of self preservation not for the region. We do not need to allege treachery in a democracy, what we need to is to get our politics right.

Essential Fidel At 85*

This week end, the retired (but intellectually ever activist Cuban revolutionary and long-time leader) Fidel Castro turns 85. Precisely on Aug 13! Fidel Castro Ruz was born on 13 Aug 1926, near Birán, Cuba. Reflecting on Fidel at 85, means an unconscious assessment of Cuban revolution at 50! Fidel Castrol became political leader of Cuba, following the historic Cuban revolution in 1959. He formally resigned from power in 2008, 50 years he together with his compatriots in the Cuban communist party transformed his country into the first socialist independent state in the Western Hemisphere from a dependent casino satellite state of United States of America. Yours sincerely once wrote that if the former President of Cuba, Fidel Castro Ruz had no "intestinal surgery" to battle with leading to his retirement in 2008, the fatigue arising from an alternative staying power in the context of a global dictatorship of one road to development (the market!) could have taken its toll on Fidel anyway. Fidel Castro was not physically imprisoned like Nelson Mandela who had historic misfortunes of spending fruitful 27 years behind the walls for fighting tyranny of Apartheid. But Fidel and his 11 million courageous and proud people have been economically and political "imprisoned" through unprecedented 50-year long economic blockade by combined forces of reaction in Washington and Europe for daring to remain different in a unipolar/unilateralist world. Paradoxically all countries of the world apart from USA and Israel have voted massively against the imposition of economic blockade against Cuba. Essential Fidel is perseverance and commitment to independence in the face of unprecedented adversities and

* August 8, 2011

overwhelming power of annihilation by a big brother up North. Last week, President Barack Obama of United States turned 50 in office. True to expectations African leaders were on line queue to Washington outdoing each other with long long letters of happy birthday wishes to the American President. *Beyond blood affinity the point cannot be overstated that the real and original first "African-American President" was Fidel Castro and not President Barack Obama.* Fidel Castro once said of Cubans; "We are a Latin-African nation….African blood flows through our veins"- Che Guevara, Fidel's comrade in revolution was in the Congo fighting with Patrice Lumumba for the liberation of Congo. In the same year (paradoxically the year Obama was born!), Cubans sent troops to back Algerian freedom fighters led by Ahmed Ben Bella. The essential features of Cuba under Fidel Castro crystal clear to Africa and Africans are unprecedented solidarity and support for Africans' struggle against colonialism, racism and hated system Apartheid, underdevelopment and crushing debt burden. Cuba sent as many as 30,000 Cuban volunteer troops to repel racist South African soldiers who were bent on undermining Angolan independence in 1976. In January 1975, the dying Portuguese colonial power was compelled to sign an agreement granting independence in November of that year following the struggle of People's Movement for the Liberation of Angola (MPLA). Desperate to stem the tide of change, given that Mozambique under Frelimo also got independence same year, the racist South Africa invaded Angola from Namibia. No independent African state was in the position to come to the rescue of Angola. Fidel's Cuba rose to the challenge and South African troops were beaten to a retreat. That singular historic Cuban resistance against South African aggression paved the way for Angolan independence in 1976. Cuba was the only frontline non-African country in the league of Tanzania, Zambia and Nigeria that felt the heat and sacrifices of liberation struggle.

Cuba was among the first countries to recognize MPLA led government and was the country that pushed for its UN membership which was ironically vetoed by United States. Africans would also remember the battle of Ciuto Cuanavale in South eastern Angola in 1987 with Cuban involvement. That historic battle against racist troops led to series of events that eventually led to Namibian independence. The value-chain of Cuban solidarity goes beyond the military. During a visit to Angola in 1977, Cuban defence minister, Raul Castro invited Angola to send 2,000 children to attend schools and universities in Cuba. Cuban doctors and nurses have served and are serving in virtually all African countries as part of comprehensive development cooperation. Today Cuba is a medical super power, thanks to Cuban revolution. In the eighties, President Shehu Shagari administration proudly hailed the Cuban doctors for their courage and sacrifices to serve in rural Nigeria scorned by Nigeria's doctors. In 2000, as many as 10,000 Cuban doctors, one third of its total doctors were serving in Africa. The same solidarity applied to education. When late Julius Nyerere of Tanzania visited the famous Isle of Youth in Cuba, an internationalist school where African youths were undergoing schooling free of charge, he reportedly said "There is no more beautiful place under the sun". A conference sponsored by the UN Special Committee against Apartheid held in Havana in May 1976. Cuban leader Armando Hart called racism the "ideology of the exploiters". That was at a time Britain and America were bursting sanctions against the outlaw regime and even talked of "constructive engagement" with the racists. Today, both the debtor- and creditors-nations were talking of partial and total debt-cancellation and debt relief. And that was precisely what Fidel Castro had long promoted in his decade-long battle of developmental ideas. He had compared the debt burden "to that torment in Greek mythology in which a man is doomed to push a large stone uphill for all eternity, a stone that always rolls down again before reaching the top." Debtors, he maintained "don't need new loans". Reason? "If Brazil is paying $12 billion a year for the interest on its debts, it doesn't need any loans; if it invested that $12 billion, it would have $120 billion for development purposes in ten years". Fidel insisted and he had since been proven right that debt was "unpayable and uncollectible". We must attribute the series of debt cancellation of the two decades to Fidel Castro and not the astuteness of negotiators and so called altruism of creditors. The world has wisely shifted to Cuban development paradigm after the scandalous market collapse of 2007 without acknowledging Fidel and Cubans who promoted the role the sate and governance in development. Cuba has the lowest HIV prevalent rate, thanks to education and non-commercialization of the battle against the scourge. Cuba ranks high on UN development index, much to its nurtured human capital through quality literacy and good health. In fact Cuba shows that the real "resource control" should start with human capital. Long Live Fidel Castro!

Bishop Hassan Kukah - Witness to Ordination*

Yours truly was among the significant diverse mass which witnessed the historic Episcopal ordination and installation of Rt Rev. Msgr Matthew Hassan Kukah as the 4th Catholic Bishop of the Sokoto Diocese at Sokoto Trade Fair Complex last Thursday (8th of September 2011). I bear witness that contrary to the artificially promoted binary constant clash of faiths and faithful in Nigeria, Bishop Kukah's ordination brought to live the reality of our advanced religious maturity and tolerance (of late under threat) as well as our potentials for sustainable religious harmony. The successful ordination of Bishop Kukah tasks us to go beyond the recent unhelpful few institutional religious and dogmatic constructions and learn to practice our blessed faiths in personal and socially relevant terms. For one as a Muslim, my activist encounter with a friend (and I dare say Comrade Bishop) spanning a decade is in the realm of social relevance. Being a witness to the ordination of Bishop Kukah is a practical reflection of the extent to which difference of religious convictions does not inhibit us from finding a common ground to collectively work for a better Nigeria. *Bishop Kukah remains a formidable social unifying capital that could bring together a remarkable mix of Nigerians regardless of their religious and political profiling.* Witness Former president, Chief Olusegun Obasanjo; ex-Head of State, General Yakubu Gowon; Secretary to the Government of the Federation, Chief Anyim Pius Anyim as well as three serving governors (Adams Oshiomhole of Edo state, Dr Kayode Fayemi of Ekiti state and Kukah's state governor Patrick Yakowa) were among

* September 12, 2011

the thousands of people who witnessed the Episcopal ordination and installation of Right Reverend Mathew Hassan Kukah as the 4th Bishop of the Sokoto Catholic diocese. I could not have imagined some hours-long gathering that could bring former Defence Minister Gen Theophilus Danjuma and former General Obasanjo together on the same podium without some unwholesome star words (indeed they stood up repeatedly in praise of God) if not Bishop Kukah's ordination. Former member of the Oputa Panel on Rights Violations and author of several chapters in books, journals and informed objective commentator on topical issues of the day had certainly touched many lives beyond the "religious". His pedigree also parades more than the "religious": alumni of the famous St. Anthony's College, University of Oxford, a Senior Rhodes fellow from 2002 to 2003, the prestigious Kennedy School of Government (KSG) Harvard University Boston, Massachusetts, Edward Mason Fellow where he bagged MA in public policy in 2004, among others. His recently launched book, on his experience in Oputal Panel, "Witness To Justice: An Insiders Account of Nigeria's Truth Commission" is a reader's delight. Bishop Kukah replaces Bishop J. Kevin Aje, following pastoral resignation. After the historic event I wondered aloud with the Mr Steve Orasanya former Head of Service of the Federation why the disconnection between our "religiosity" and our wars of attrition for the occupation of national political space. If Bishops do resign, why would our politicians sit so tight? If succession plan was as elegant and smooth as witnessed at the Diocese of Sokoto, why are we weighed down by legal overloads, rigged elections and pure electoral robberies during elections that are expected to ensure smooth political succession? However profound appreciation must go to the Sokoto caliphate under the leadership of Sultan of Sokoto, Alhaji Sa'ad Abubakar III, for presiding over an environment of faith pluralism and tolerance. The Diocese of Sokoto came into existence in 1964. Catholics are certainly few compared to scores of mass of millions of Muslims. Yet that the Dioceses could pursue their faith unmolested puts to lie the media smear that casts Muslim community as a "protective hothouse".

Monsignor Kukah reportedly left a great legacy as the vicar-general of the Kaduna archdiocese as well as the parish priest of St.

Andrew Catholic Church, Kakuri, Kaduna. There is no doubt that he will make a difference as the new Bishop of Sokoto Diocese. As a tested and broadminded cleric, many Nigerians regardless of faiths are confident that he will make a positive difference to promote unity of faiths against the social ills of Nigeria and above all deepen the similarities of faiths with respect to Godliness, love, honesty, respect and dignity of humanity. The critical question however is whether the new Bishop will sustain his social commentary in the light his new pastoral challenges? His recent extensive interview with *Africa Confidential* in London about the prospects for political change and economic reform in the run-up to last year's elections remains a food for thought and a compulsory read for those who want to fully appreciate the elevation of a "peoples' Bishop"!

Worthy Honours - Yar'Adua and Professor Gambari*

The premier University of Ibadan (UI) marks its 63rd Foundation Day this week, precisely Thursday 17th of November, 2011. A significant feature of the pack of landmark activities for the historic occasion is the award of posthumous degrees of letter to the late President Umaru Yar'Adua and Professor Ibrahim Gambari, Under-Secretary General and Special Adviser on Africa to the United Nations (UN) Secretary-General and two other eminent Nigerians. The News Agency of Nigeria (NAN) quoted the official statement from UI as saying that the recipients are being honoured for their contributions to educational development and social re-engineering in the country. As an old proverb has it; "Honour shows the man". The historic honours for both Professor Ibrahim A. Gambari and the late President Yar'Adua by UI once again bring to the fore the bagful of values both have added (and still adding in the case of Gambari) to humanity. With specific reference to late President Yar'Adua, the statement said Yar'Adua deserved the honour, "because he appropriated funds for the opening up of the second phase of UI, Ajibode, which is going to accommodate further development of the university." UI management is absolutely right to single out one mark of statesmanship of the late President with direct bearing to the expansion of the premier university. This singular UI recognition only unlocks the remarkable legacy of Yar'Adua during his brief spell as the President. Yours truly has once argued that since the late Prime Minister, Tafawa Balewa and Alhaji Shehu Shagari, the late President

* November 14, 2011

Umaru Musa Yar'Adua deserved the credit for returning civility to Federal governance. Not few Presidents (including one military prototype) had acted philosopher-kings interpreting Nigerian reality with boring words, (spoken but not meant). His prompt and quite appropriation of outstanding funds for the expansion of UI is a typical feature of his civility and above all knowledge driven governance style. Many thanks to the leadership of UI for acknowledging the contribution of Yar'Adua to humanity in the area of investment in education. The inaugural address of the late President on May 29th 2007 was refreshingly brief. For the mass of Nigerians, Yar'Adua did the unprecedented: he did not increase products' price at all but rather reduced the price from 70 to 65 naira per litre. The dividend of Yar'Adua's civility for the nation was relative industrial peace since 2007 up to when he died in office. In three years Obasanjo administration arbitrarily marked up prices almost four times, with attendant national strikes. Conversely Yar'Adua's administration did not record a single national strike beyond the one planted for him by departing OBJ. Only President Shehu Shagari's administration dared to parallel Yar'Adua's record in industrial harmony. In place of policy dictatorship of OBJ, Yar'Adua institutionalized social dialogue as distinct from criminalization as means of engagement with labour. Yar'Adua elected to be a "servant leader" who will be a "listener" and "doer" and "serve with humility". Precious things come in small packages", so goes the popular marketing wisdom. Just by a stroke of presidential gesture and surprise, late President Yar'Adua made public his declared assets to the Code of Conduct Bureau.He qualitatively elevated the anti-corruption discourse more than the pedestrian and the symbolic disaster/public relations/media mess of the past and the current dispensation. By a singular force of example, late President Yar'Adua shifted the partial dim probity searchlight from some few others to a full blown beam on all public holders including him. Lagos State federation money was promptly refunded following a correct interpretation of the Supreme Court judgment. After his death, we have come to know that what the nation needs desperately are soft leadership issues, namely integrity, peace, dialogue and engagement. Witness Niger Delta too in which unprecedented official engagement with aggrieved citizens led to improved oil production in the region and restored hope for development.

UI's recognition of Professor Ibrahim A. Gambari, further confirms his pedigree as a true scholar-diplomat. He was appointed by the United Nations Secretary-General Ban Ki-moon and the Chairperson of the African Union Commission, Jean Ping, as Joint Special Representative of the Africa Union-United Nations Hybrid Operation in Darfur, effective 1 January 2010. The only African to be so charged with global responsibility and with reposed confidence. Professor Gambari was once Under-Secretary-General and Special Adviser to the Secretary-General on the Iraq Compact and Other Issues from 2007 to 2009. On 22 May 2007, the Secretary-General entrusted him with the Good Offices Mandate on Myanmar. Mr. Gambari was also Under- Secretary-General for Political Affairs, from 2005 to 2007; UN Special Adviser on Africa (1999-2005), and Special Representative of the Secretary-General and Head of the United Nations Mission to Angola (2002-2003). Before joining the United Nations, he served his country as Ambassador and Permanent

Representative of Nigeria to the United Nations (1990-1999). In this position, Mr. Gambar chaired the United Nations Special Committee against Apartheid. He was also Minister of Foreign Affairs of Nigeria (1984-1985), and before that the Director-General of the Nigerian Institute of International Affairs. He is the author of several books and scholarly articles. Mr. Gambari is a recipient in 2002 of the national honour, Commander of the Federal Republic of Nigeria (CFR). He has also been awarded Doctor of Humane Letters degree (honoris causa) from the University of Bridgeport Connecticut (2002), Fairleigh Dickinson University, New Jersey (2006) and an Honorary Doctorate of Public Service degree from Chatham University (May 2008). Others include the Special Recognition for International Development and Diplomacy award conferred by the Africa-America Institute (September 2007), the Distinguished (Foreign) Service Award by the Federal Government of Nigeria (April 2008), the Harry Edmonds Award for Lifetime Achievement (May 2009) and the Campaign Against Genocide Medal by the Republic of Rwanda (July 2010). UI truly has two global citizens on its list of honours.

Quotable Ojukwu*

There are scores of received wisdoms about human attitude to the dead. Such as; "Never speak ill of the dead", a maxim reportedly attributed to the Spartan philosopher, Chilo of the sixth century BC.

This perhaps explains the bagful of bi-partisan positive commentaries on Chief Emeka Odumegwu-Ojukwu who died recently in London after a protracted illness. Even at that I search in vain for some received wisdoms about sycophancy about the dead until torrents of tributes came in for Ikemba, a former warlord turned activist politician. Witness for instance, the former governor of Ekiti State, Chief Segun Oni, who described the death of Ikemba of Nnewi, Chief Chukwuemeka Odumegwu Ojukwu, as the fall of "the biggest iroko tree in the forest of Igboland." And reportedly he said that in Ibo language too for those who care; "oke osisi di na nukwu ogha na ala igbo adawoo". Chief Oni never availed all us other iroko trees in Igboland to prove the validity of his attributions to Ikemba. For the Northern governors Nigeria "has lost a great son". The chairman of the forum, who is also the governor of Niger State, Dr Mu'azu Babangida Aliyu, said the people of Niger State, the 19 states of the North and, indeed, the entire country had lost a courageous man, who would be missed for his immeasurable contributions to national development. For Fashola Lagos State governor, the death of the late Ikemba of Nnewi, Chief Odumegwu Ojukwu, was a big personal loss to him personally and to Nigerians generally. According to him "though, we knew his health has been poor, one still expected a miracle from somebody whose image was as large as who he was as the Ikemba of Nnewi." According to Action Congress of Nigeria

---

* Daily Trust, 5th December, 2011

(ACN) the death of Emeka Odumegwu-Ojukwu, "robs Nigeria of a veritable voice of wisdom at a critical time in the country's history."

They constitute truly quotable Ojukwu.

ON ZIK

"He was the indefatigable fighter for freedom and equality. To all intents and purposes, Zik inserted the word 'politics' into my life's dictionary. I respected, I worshipped, I considered him a hero, and saw him as a living legend. In my own candid opinion, Zik did not set out to lead the Igbo and has not in fact led the Igbo. He has been first and foremost a Nigerian who aspired to a Nigerian leadership. As a father, I love and respect him. As a politician, I disagree with his policies."

On Chief Obafemi Awolowo

"As a leader of the modern cast, he has left Nigeria standards which are indelible, standards beside which future aspirations to public leadership can be eternally measured. He was a brilliant political administrator and a most erudite teacher. At his death I had the singular honour of proposing for him this epitaph that has endured — 'he was the best President that Nigeria never had.'

On Sir Ahmadu Bello

"Whenever children, the heirs of our today, read the history of Nigeria, the one name that must command admiration and one which will, without doubt, attract the largest fan club would be that of Sir Ahmadu Bello, Sardauna of Sokoto. Here was a man every inch a prince who bestrode the Nigeria of his days and won, if not admiration, then the respect of friends and foes alike. Here was a man who roused the sleeping giant of the North from its centuries-old slumber and within the short span of six years placed it in a dominant position in Nigeria. He laid the foundations of a northern pre-eminence in Nigeria that has lasted until today and which threatens to last into a future without limit. Everything Sir Ahmadu believed, he believed sincerely. He understood his people and inspired them to heights which they never appeared to think possible. As a leader, he was superb and very successful."

On Yakubu Gowon

"People make me laugh when they talk about an enmity between Yakubu Gowon and Ojukwu. That Gowon and I did not see eye to eye on certain issue was as a result of our different perceptions of the situation at the time. These were perceptions built into our being in Nigeria. In leading the war we both postured. For anyone, therefore, to try and extend this posturing and make it permanent on the national stage, to my mind, is sterile. I will most certainly invite Gowon to my house for lunch any day."

On Hajiya Gambo

"Hajia Gambo is a veritable revolution all within herself. For as long she can remember, she has been part of the struggle and for as long as anyone cares to remember, Bambo Sawaba has been part of the struggle. The British colonial authority noted her stubbornness and fearlessness in the anti-colonial struggle."

On Gani Fawehinmi

"Whenever a final history of this country of ours is written, I am sure that the name of Gani Fawehinmi would merit a prominent passage. Gani symbolises, perhaps, the very best of professionalism in an epoch where everything including the intellectualism is up for sale to the highest bidder. Where other lawyers are content to win cases, Gani's aim remains to employ his very extensive knowledge of law to ensure justice. To him fees are of a minor consideration. "Yet, there can be no doubt that Nigeria is better off with the courageous crusade of this lone-ranger".

Bade Onimode - Remembering *the Afro-optimist*[*]

On Saturday December 10th, I faced a dilemma of two invitations for double historic memorials, namely 10th Memorial Colloquium in Honour of Professor Bade Onimode in Lokoja and the 1st Shehu Musa Yar'Adua Memorial Lecture in Abuja at the Shehu Musa Yar'Adua Center. If you tolerate my ideological bias, apart from my interest in listening to President Jacob Zuma of South Africa who was the Special Guest of Honour at Abuja memorial (with the hope of having a feel of what is left of his passion for Africa and alternative development) my ideological preference was for Lokoja memorial scheduled to parade notable radical African thinkers like, Professor Ben Turok, Member of Parliament of South Africa, Professor Etannibi Alemika of University of Jos, Professor Olorode of University of Abuja, Comrade Hassan Sunmonu, Secretary General of Organization of African Trade Unity (OATUU), Dr Peter Ozo-Ezon of NLC and yours comradely among others. Thank God that I witnessed the two memorials in good measure; Abuja and Lokoja in-that-order. Professor Bade Onimode was born in November 1944 and died in 2001, some 57 years. He was a possibly the last African optimistic political economist after the late Professor Claude Ake and Afro-optimist- historian Dr Bala Usman, of University of Port Harcourt and ABU Zaria respectively. Professor Onimode studied economics at the University of Ibadan between September 1963 and September 1967 when he got his first degree and proceeded immediately for his Masters degree in economics in the same University. He later got another master degree in 1969 at

[*] December 19, 2011

the University of Chicago and PhD at the Ohio State University in 1972. The political economist was the Chairman of the then Association of University Teachers (now Academic Staff Union of Universities), University of Ibadan Branch between 1977 and 1978 during the Ali Must Go mass protest by Nigerian students against the first and the most notorious anti poor/education policies of the General Obasanjo military government. He was one of the lecturers that were victimised and repressed as a result of their active participation in that mass *occupy* the campus protests. Prof. Onimode was the pioneer Chairman of the London based Institute for African Alternatives (IFAA) from 1986 to 1996; served as member of the Eminent Persons Committee of the Economic Community of West African States (ECOWAS); one time member of the Scientific Advisory Board of the African Centre for Development and Strategic Studies; and Vice Chairman for West Africa on the Board of the African Economic and Social Research Forum of the defunct Organisation of African Unity (OAU). Between 1997 and 1999, Prof. Onimode was the Deputy Vice Chancellor (Academics) of the University of Ibadan and member of the Governing Council of the University of Lagos from 2000 until he died in 2001. A Life Fellow of the Nigerian Economic Society, Professor Onimode was also a member of the Research Review Committee of the United Nations Institute for Development Planning (IDEP) from 1992 to 1998. He consulted extensively for several local and international organisations, including the International Labour Organisation (ILO), the United Nations Economic Commission on Africa (ECA). The late Professor was a prolific author on African *Development, Development and Development* (ad ifinitum) and please note not on *Corruption or reform* being the new neo-liberal passing fads for underdevelopment. Witness his intellectual outputs at record time of his relatively short-span; *Imperialism and Underdevelopment in Nigeria (1983); A Political Economy of the African Crisis (1988), The IMF, the World Bank and the African Debt (1989); A Future for Africa – Beyond the Politics of Adjustment (1992); Issues in African Development (1995); Africa in the World of the 21st Century (2000).* The testimony by Professor Ben Turok about Professor Bade Onimode entitled as " a GIANT OF AFRICA" sums up who Bade was:

"I have no doubt whatsoever that Bade Onimode was one of the most outstanding African intellectuals of our times. The continent has yet to fully recognise his contributions to our understanding of economics but that is due to the failure to shift away from the dominant neoliberal paradigm and not because Onimode failed to present a sound theoretical alternative."

His last book entitled; *Africa in the World of the 21st Century (2000)* is a compulsory read for African pessimists including African Heads of States who confronted their citizens with policy blackmail of TINA (There Is No Alternative) to devaluation, liberalization, privatization and (the latest Jonathan government policy blackmail); subsidy removal. Onimode saw Africa as a land of development opportunities not official despair stories and poverty generating policies imposed by IMF and World Bank. According to him:

"In other regions of the World, regional economic blocs such as the European Union (EU), NAFTA in North America, and ASEAN in the Pacific Rim have been established and revamped for the global competition of the new century. National institutions such as airlines, shipping lines, military-industrial complexes, transnational corporations, etc have also been renovated for the global contests of the twenty-first century. Unviable institutions and structures have been eliminated, merged or rationalized for the anticipated keen competition of the century. Africa shows few parallel responses in these ways to the mounting international euphoria about the century.

It is tempting to yield to the seductive argument that those who cannot get three square meals at present cannot be expected to bother about the new century. This feeling then tends to concentrate all attention on the daunting problems of the present – poverty, external debt, failed SAPs, conflicts, environmental degradation, marginalisation and the like. These are quite compelling and legitimate concerns.

But our strategies for dealing with the problems of the present must be informed, both by the lesson of the past (and of the other parts of the world) as well as our expectations about future developments. Africa has no choice but to develop in its own way with the rest of the world; it must therefore strive to understand that world, its future directions, challenges and opportunities."

Professor Ben Turok said it all about Nigeria and Bade Onimode:

> "There is certainly something about Nigeria's capacity to produce extraordinary personalities, though the continent as a whole has yet to acknowledge that properly. Perhaps Nigeria does not publish enough or make it available across the continent. Perhaps the turbulent political environment makes people uneasy. I do not know the answer, but I am always mystified about the inadequate recognition of your (read; Nigeria's) immense vitality and capabilities as a country."

Will somebody give Professor Bade Onimode a posthumous legitimate and earned national honour please?

Ojukwu - Farewell to *arms*[*]

Blessed are the dead, for they shall never be suspected, so goes the received wisdom. Blessed is the late ex-Biafran warlord, Dim Chukwuemeka Odumegwu Ojukwu who was buried last weekend. Whatever the controversy around the legacy of *Dim* Ojukwu, he would henceforth no more be suspected of electricity shortages, road accidents, carpet crossing, serial security challenges, soil erosion, kidnappings, political violence and all that add up to the bagful of negativities in Nigeria's recent reactionary narrative. Just as other notable fallen compatriots such as late Professor Sam Aluko would no longer be made to explain our perennial crisis of governance. Ojukwu and other dead compatriots carry no burden of Nigeria's challenge to meet the Millennium Development Goals in less than three years. They could care less either if we are part of the league of 20 developed economies in 2020 or the miserable pack of rich nations, poor peoples. Let the truth be told; it is we the living mourners, including the recent month-long genuine and emergency sympathizers alike who truly need the prayers and empathy to carry on from the mess Ojukwu, late warlord left Nigeria and Nigerians in spite of his modest mark and that of other fallen compatriots. We are the ones that must make elections free and fair and credible. Anambra State Governor, Mr Peter Obi would go down in history as a worthy chief/host mourner at Ojukwu's concluded burial. He has commendably taken up this post humous challenge of life after Ojukwu. At the burial of Ojukwu on friday, Peter Obi hit the nail on the head. He elevated the burial narrative of Dim beyond the sentimental when he said that; "*the Nigerian civil war has finally ended with the burial of in his Nnewi country*

[*] *Daily Trust*, March 5, 2012

home". Most tributes to the late Biafra leader were written with an eye on some kind of cheap *political correctness.* Some tributes were sheer expressions of plain political opportunism (witness my friend, Chief servant of Niger state, Governor Muazum who said he could have travelled same road, the road *Dim* Odumegwu Ojukwu did not recommend for anybody while he was alive). Very few statesmen and women made profound tributes with an eye on bigger picture of nation- building of Nigeria and Africa. Exceptionally but understandably unique however was that of Bianca, the standing widow of the chief Emeka. Her 1000 plus love words provoked the nostalgia of the flirtatious games between Henry and Catherine *in* Ernest Hemingway's *A Farewell to Arms.* Bianca, Ikemba's wife for 23 years certainly has the legitimate monopoly right of saying it all, "you were my husband, my brother, my friend, my child. I was your queen, and it was an honour to have served you." But beyond the privatized two arms of Ikemba *the other arms* were those freely exchanged by the Biafra and federal sides of the unfortunate divide in some 30 bloody months, (1967 to 1970. At the last count as many as 100,000 soldiers died and over a million civilians, (most of the latter of which tragically perished of starvation under an imposed blockade with no benefits of dignified burials). Governor Peter Obi refreshingly but constructively acknowledged the national and global significance of the befitting funeral for the late Ojukwu; a *farewell to arms* (of mass destruction!) and a formal end of the tragic avoidable civil war during which hitherto brothers and sisters unacceptably turned against each other in war of attrition. According to Peter Obi, the love showed the Ojukwu family and entire Ndigbo by President Goodluck Jonathan and indeed all Nigerians was an indication that the discrimination suffered by Ndigbo after the civil war was over. Ibos he said can now have a sense of belonging in the Nigerian project that awaits us. Yours sincerely holds that three decades after the quotable Gowon; *"no victor, no vanquished*", Obi's remark is the most refreshingly profound and statesmanlike. Peter Obi's statement is the only quotable quote in the volume of trillion of printed tributes to the late chieftain. His statement touched on the heart of the matter; *nation building compared to* President Jonathan who reportedly said among others that Ikemba's burial was "personal" to him". The import of

Obi's observation according to which Ikemba's burial marked the end of civil war cannot be overstated. For one Obi's remark once again confirms the resilience of Nigeria and Nigerians to dance out of the brink in the face of testy challenges of nation building. Much had been written about the great reconciliation in South Africa under the great leadership of Nelson Mandela following the global defeat of the hated inhuman Apartheid white regime. But lest we forget so soon, *Nigeria and Nigerians first invented the words; "Reconciliation, Reconstruction, and Rehabilitation (in that order) after the civil war ended 13th of January 1970, South Africans only copied us.* As Peter Obi pointed out the outpour of sympathy and solidarity for Ikemba was an anti-climax of the great capacity of Nigerians to move ahead in the great task of sustaining Nigerian project. Secondly, the bi-partisan pan Nigerian standstill for the late Odumegwu Ojukwu has exposed the theoretical fallacy of the proponents of the so-called Sovereign national conference. At the end of the day, we are certainly not a divided nation after all. Nigeria is not (and should not) be a debating society. When we want to bury our dead, (heroes or villains alike), we mobilize and get it done. We must do the same to generate electricity for reindustrialization. We must have a similar bi-partisan mobilization to banish poverty, create mass jobs, halt terrorism, ensure free and fair elections and rebuild public schools. In nutshell let us be a productive country rather than an endless debating society. A day after Ojukwu's burial the real tribute must go former President Shehu Shagari. He turned 87 recently. *Shagari was the President with larger heart (who Nelson Mandela must have emulated in the art of forgiveness and seeing the bigger picture!). Notwithstanding the partisan pressures within his party, NPN and the opposition parties notably Zik's NPP he nonetheless with political sagacity navigated the delicate historic balance by pardoning both former Lt Colonel Ojukwu and General Gowon.* He courageously struck off their names from the "wanted list" and allowed home from exile to keep up adding value. Nigeria has a lot to certainly teach the war-torn world in the art of compromise, peace building, dialogue and reconciliation. But that is if we resist the temptation of those who want to again undermine Nigerian project both from within and abroad.

Essential Comrade Pascal Bafyau

The remains of the 3rd elected President of Nigeria Labour Congress (NLC), Comrade Pascal Bafyau would be commuted to mother earth this weekend at his home town, Larmurde, Adamawa state. Comrade Pascal died at the age of 65 years in Abuja on Tuesday may 15th 2012.

Nigeria's labour market actors; *labour leaders, unionists in general, employers and government officials* alike received the sad news of the sudden departure of Comrade Pascal Bafyau with shock. His death with deafening big bang is a big loss to the nation's Labour Movement. The celebrated quotable quote of President Barack Obama during his historic visit to Ghana in 2008 still captures imagination; "*Africa doesn't need strongmen, it needs strong institutions*". With struggles spanning over three decades in defence of working people, NLC has truly "*come of age*" as a pan African (and indeed global) strong institution. And that is in spite of the cowardly dissolutions of its duly democratically constituted organs by military regimes of Murtala/Obasanjo, (1975) Ibrahim Babangida (1988) and Sanni Abacha (1994) (in that order of undemocratic meddlesomeness in labour affairs!). NLC interestingly has also been driven by elected men who in their respective rights at different historic contexts brought to bear their globally acknowledged energies to shape the movement on the path of service delivery to working women and men. The Presidents of NLC to date are comrades; Hassan Sunmonu (1979-1984), Ali Chiroma (1984-1988), Paschal Bafyau (1988-1994), Adams Oshiomhole (1999-2007) and Omar Abdul Waheed. The history of NLC shows that strongmen (no less strong women) as well as strong institutions are far from being mutually exclusive. The perception of the labour movement as a product of strong men (often not women) is however hardly useful in understanding the complex reality of a democratic labour movement such as NLC.

Undoubtedly, every serious labour leader brings to bear his determination, knowledge and courage. Yet leader-centred analysis says little about the logic of collective actions or inactions that characterise the daily struggles of ordinary men and women in the trade unions. The real challenge therefore lies in coming to terms with the labour movement at varying historic moments.

Whether by divine accident or divine design, almost all the former Presidents attended the last 2012 May Day lecture. With the benefit of post humus insight, the real star of this year's May Day "grounding" was comrade Paschal Bafyau. I could not recollect when last I saw Comrade Pascal at NLC May Day manifestations since his tenure was arbitrarily terminated by Abacha led military dictatorship in 1994. But there he did, without premonition it was a farewell May Day. It was an organisational loss to my union, which at its 10th Delegates Conference in Asaba, Delta state March this year honoured him with Labour Service Award, in company of other past and current Presidents. He was enthusiastic to attend but for his failing health. Comrade Pascal Bafyau as General Secretary of Nigeria Union of Railwaymen (NUR) was elected President of NLC in 1988 after the exit of the military imposed Michael Abiodun. He was re-elected in 1992. Just like his predecessor, (comrade Ali Chiroma), he presided over the NLC during serial undemocratic non-developmentalist military regimes that violated human and trade union rights with unprecedented impunity. His tenure was arbitrarily terminated by the Abacha military dictatorship when the regime dissolved the National Executive Councils (NECs) of the NLC, NUPENG and PENGASSAN in 1994 under the notorious Decrees 9 and 10. Regardless of the controversies that trailed his stewardship at NLC, (notably in engagement with the military) comrade Pascal Bafyau left behind a united labour movement. His achievements have been well documented by the NLC. He came out as an institutional comrade that presided over the building of the 12-Storey Labour House in Abuja, restructured the unions through voluntary mergers, established Labour Transport Service (now Labour City Transport), founded defunct Labour Bank (LACON), established labour Party in 1989 and united two factions of the NLC, the Democrats and Progressives. He held various positions in socially relevant institutions that added value to the promotion of the economic advancement of Nigerian people; Board Chairman of the National Mass Education Commission from 2009, Board member of the Urban Development Bank (UDBN), Nigeria Agricultural Land Development Authority (NALDA), Nigerian Social Insurance Trust Fund (NSITF) and initiated first Workers" education Endowment fund. *His greatest legacy was the dismantling of the age long disconnect between economic struggles and political struggles of trade unions. Comrade Pascal Bafyau was among the first generation of politically conscious labour leaders* daring all the risks associated with murky state/political/partisan terrains. He was a Member of the 1986 Political Bureau and the 1987 Constituent Assembly under the military regime. Pascal name possibly featured more in reports on state-labour relations than any comrade. He championed the formation and registration of the Labour party. The military regime through subterfuge deliberately raised the bar to exclude democratic forces such as the labour party from the political space. He offered to be late Chief Moshood Abiola;s running mate in the defunct Social Democratic Party (SDP). Interrogate the quality of Pascal's politics, but everybody acknowledges that he was politically audacious and not partisanship shy. With ease he traversed most contemporary political parties. His friendship was genuinely bipartisan and ideologically cross-cutting. The Labour movement truly lost a mobile political memory/library. He was a pioneer labour member of the prestigious National Institute, Kuru Jos Alumni of SEC 7/1985. Like his contemporaries such as SOZ Ejorfor, Frank Kokori, Ali Chiroma, Adams Oshiomhole, Yahaya Hashim, Lawson Osaigie, Salisu Muhammed, late Dr Lasisi Osunde, late Ogbonna, late Paul Ekpu and other notable labour leaders, he came through as a stateless, detribalized worthy global citizen. He was an internationalist well before globalization was hijacked by capital and capitalism and returned us back to our villages albeit as consumers. The sense of loss of yours comradely is more than partial; I was privileged to have him as the chairman of my wedding reception in Lagos in August 1990. He humorously presided over the cake-feeding, notwithstanding our ideological disagreement. Comrade Pascal undoubtedly struggled for good governance which sadly by and large eluded him (and indeed still eludes) Nigeria and Nigerians. South

African poet B M Themba once observed that "*Blessed are the dead, For they will; Never be suspected*". Blessed is comrade Pascal Bafyau; he will no longer be suspected of perennial electricity failure, water shortages, collapse of buildings, pension scam, mutually assured destructive serial bombings, petroleum subsidy serial mess and all that fill our over-flown bagful of bad-governance. May God make his grave spacious enough for eternal comfort!

Mandela at 94*

On 18 July 2012 Africa's Nelson Rolihlahla Madiba Mandela turned 94. Coincidentally it was in 1994 that the living legend became the President of South Africa after spending 27 years in prison.

That the Mandela brand is highly sought after by leaders, celebrities and commoners across the world is an understatement. A key part of his attraction is that he has remained unfazed by his global adulation and popularity. As Bill Clinton, former President of the US recently told the CBS News: "I don't think he [Mandela]] wanted to be a hero…I think he wanted to lead his country into freedom and unity and it was heroic and when the price turned out to be very high he just kept paying it."

For a continent where much of the world does not seem to expect anything good to come from, Mandela is a negation of that myth and an affirmation of the possibilities that Africa holds – if only it can get its act together. This is one of the main reasons why the entire Africa ought to be in the vanguard of celebrating Mandela day, which is now done globally on July 18 of every year.

Born on 18 July 1918 in the tiny village of Mvezo on the banks of the Mbashe River in the province of Transkei, 'Rolihlahla' (which in Mandela's native Xhosa language literally means 'pulling the branch of a tree' or figuratively means 'troublemaker') was named Nelson by his teacher. In 1942 he joined the African National Congress and for 20 years was involved in a campaign of peaceful, non-violent defiance against the South African government and its racist policies. With the non-violent methods of the struggle doing little to convince the racist regime to repent from its evil ways and

---

* *Daily Trust*, July 30, 2012

repeal its obnoxious policies, Mandela became increasingly radicalised and became a co-founder of Umkhonto we Sizwe, the armed wing of the African National Congress (ANC). He was arrested in 1962 and convicted of sabotage and other charges. He served 27 years in prison, many of these in the notorious Robben Island. He was offered release several times on the condition that the ANC would renounce violence as an instrument of struggle. He declined the Greek gift on each occasion. Following his eventual release from prison on 11 February 1990, Mandela led his party in the negotiations that led to the establishment of democracy in South Africa in 1994, with himself as the first President of post-Apartheid South Africa. As President, he frequently gave priority to reconciliation, while introducing policies aimed at combating poverty and inequality in South Africa.

It is remarkable that though Mandela was the President of South Africa from 1994 to 1999, he is less remembered for his presidency than for the enduring legacy he left by his unique ability to forgive those who jailed him for 27 years and for being a symbol of reconciliation in a nation polarized along ethnic, racial and class cleavages. Though South Africa still remains a polarized country, the Mandela brand has become a metaphor linking all the polarities in the country together and somehow reminding each of the contending elements of the virtues of sacrifice, forgiveness and reconciliation. This is his greatest legacy to South Africa in particular and to mankind in general.

To celebrate this year's Mandela Day, the United Nations launched a campaign asking people to mark the day by devoting 67 minutes of their time to helping others – one minute for each year Mandela spent fighting for his cause. In South Africa, the Department of Basic Education in partnership with the Nelson Mandela Centre of Memory, Brand South Africa and several partners in education on 10 April 2012 launched the 94+ Schools Infrastructure Project – to make a little difference in the education sector in honour of Madiba. The Mandela Day aims at inspiring people to set aside some minutes to consciously do something that will help change the world or their environment for the better, and by so doing to become part of a global movement of people consciously aspiring to do good. Curiously while the rest of the world celebrates the Mandela Day, not much was heard from the Nigerian government about this living legend on July 18.

At 94, Mandela may be too frail to celebrate or entertain us with the famous 'Mandelaic' rollicking dance steps but in popular imagination he remains strong, ever optimistic, ever forgiving and ever reconciling. Put simply Mandela is among the few people in the world who have achieved immortality in their life time and who know that history will be kind to them even after they have long returned to their Maker.

Femi Falana: in praise of Principles*

The Friends of Femi Falana (FFF) group (which happily include yours comradely) celeberates Mr Femi Falana for his recent elevation to the rank of the Senior Advocate of Nigeria (SAN) with some intellectual grounding of activists and comrades in Ibadan, Oyo State. Professor Chidi Odinkalu Chairman, Human Rights Commission (HRC) leads a discussion on the Justiciability of the Social Economic Rights in Nigeria; Reflections on the contributions of Femi Falana. An activist lawyer, a patriot and globally acknowledged human rights campaigner, Femi Falana in his own right has always been a senior advocate of Nigeria and indeed Africa anyday. The recent elevation of the human rights activist alongside 24 others to the elite lawyers' rank of Senior Advocates of Nigeria, SAN, by the Legal Practitioners Privileges committee only formalises what has been long expected and what has always been anyway. In many aspects I share a lot in common with Femi Falana.

For one, we are all proud children of Independent Nigeria. Mr Falana was born on 20 May 1958 at Ilawe, Ekiti state, Nigeria, two years before the British flag was lowered and replaced with Green-White-Green Nigerian flag. He had his primary schooling at St. Michael's Primary School, Ilawe, between 1963 and 1970. His secondary education was at Sacred Heart Catholic Seminary between 1971 and 1975. He proceeded to the Nigeria Law School, Lagos in 1981 and was called to the bar in 1982. This was indeed a remarkable upward uninterrupted educational mobility of young Femi from relatively ground zero in 1963 to a qualified Anthony of the Federal Republic in 1981.

---

* *Daily Trust*, December 10, 2012

With the type of Independence children like Femi Falana, yours truly, Sanusi Lamidos and all other 1950s, who then dare interrogate the benefits of the struggle for independence which featured nationalist heroes like Chief Obafemi Awolowo, Sir Ahmadu Bello and great Zik of Africa, Nmadi Azikwe? Colonialist Lugardian Nigeria built no public primary and secondary schools much less a University and a law school that would throw up the likes of Femi Falana. Walter Rodney was right when he wrote that colonialism had only one hand-'It was a one armed bandit'. Our great fathers under the heel of colonialism were deliberately denied education that post independent Nigeria generously offered to us. The lesson; no alternative to Independence.

After the compulsory national youth service, he joined the Chambers of Alao Aka-Bashorun, a renowned progressive legal activist and patriot. Femi could not have elected to serve in another chambers. Aka Bashorun legal Chambers at Jebba West in Lagos for almost four decades was the Nigeria's equivalent of legendary Mandela-Oliver legal office at Fox street Johannesburg which opened doors to justice and fairness for the oppressed and under privileged. Jebba West was a market place of ideas and activities for freedom, anti-Apartheid, democracy and socialism, perceived then as "subversion" by the status quo. Aka Bashorun was a meticulous lawyer who shared traditions with famous progressive lawyers who put law at the service of the oppressed such as South Africa's late Yusuf Dadoo, Alfred Nzo, Nelson Mandela and Oliver Tambo. Though a far more junior partner, he was de facto a co-comrade of the late Aka Bashorun on account of audacity of hope for a progressive Nigeria. Femi Falana has always been a good follower which explains why he is a tested leader of the civil society today. In 1991, Mr Falana started his own Chambers, Femi Falana, which later became Falana and Falana Chambers.

Femi Falana became a human rights activist as early as 1983 for which he has paid heavy price in terms undeserved harassements and detentions especially under the military. For instance, just for standing up for the defence of students' rights Mr Falana was almost denied his discharge certificate by the National Youth Service Corps

(NYSC). Two decades later, in July 2001, he petitioned the Justice Oputa led human rights panel over his withheld certificate. The certificate was subsequently released to him on live television at the commission's sitting.

Femi has presided over the affairs of the National Association of Democratic Lawyers and West African Bar Association, WABA President and Chairman respectively. He legitimately contested and lost the governorship election of Ekiti State in 2007 on the ticket of the National Conscience Party. Falana is qualified to be called a statesman. Though a visible non-state actor, very few statesmen have shown such passion for nation-building in terms of advocacy, legal representation and mass engagement. Just like the late Aka Bashrun and Chief Gani Fawehinmi. Femi who also features at next year's Daily Trust Dialogue proudly gave out his first daughter Winnie (born at the height of anti- Apartheid struggles of the 80s and named after Winnie Mandela) to marriage last saturday in Lagos in an event that witnessed a remarkable collection of all those committed to a better world. Falana truly stands for something (principle) which explains why he does not fall for anything as many are doing. The unstinting commitment to humanity is undoubtedly the fundamental principle that Falana holds dearly.

Patrick Ibrahim Yakowa: A Tribute*

Like most compatriots, I received with great shock and deep grief, the death of His Excellency, the Executive Governor of Kaduna State, Sir Patrick Ibrahim Yakowa, in a helicopter crash at Nembe-Okoroba area of Bayelsa State. The crash claimed other notables that included former National Security Adviser (NSA), General Andrew Azazi (rtd) among others on Saturday December 15, 2012.

The dramatic elevations of Dr Goodluck Jonathan, Namadi Sambo GCON and Patrick Ibrahim Yakowa as President, Vice President of the Federal Republic of Nigeria and Governor of Kaduna State respectively, following the death of the former President Musa Yar'Adua were manifestations of the triumph of our democratic process, despite its enormous challenges.

Their respective elevations must have then very well magnified the political fortunes of the three but the real credit goes to democracy and our constitutionalism.

The fact that Nigeria could do a transition with all the challenges both at the federal and state levels indicates that we are really coming of age as democratic people and nation. All we need to do is to nurture this democratic process and not undermine it. Alas the sudden death of Yakowa further tasks our commitment and resolve to deepen democracy through peaceful transition process.

With his death, my union (National Union of Textile workers) has particularly lost a voice for re-industrialization of the North in general and revival of textile industry in Kaduna in particular. He was among the few standing governors making a case of industry in the North.

---

* *Daily Trust*, 17th December 2012

Speaking at the 10th Quadrennial National Delegates' Conference (NDC) of the National Union of Textile, Garment and Tailoring Workers of Nigeria (NUTGTWN) in Asaba, the Delta State capital, in early this year, the governor demanded for a concerted effort by all Nigerians to return the industry to pre-1987 boom.

Disturbed by the high rate of smuggling of textile materials to the country, which has adversely affected indigenous production, Yakowa argued that the situation had reduced patronage on made in Nigeria textile.

The governor, who was represented by the Deputy Governor, Muktar Ramalan Yero (who was sworn in yesterday as governor) expressed concern that the textile industry which was once the highest employer of labour in Nigeria was gradually becoming moribund due to impact of smuggling. His death is an organizational loss to our union which at our Delegates Conference in Asaba March this year honoured him with *Industry-Friendly* Award with a subsequent courtesy call by the new leadership of the union.

As a Deputy Governor of Kaduna State under the administration of Architect Namadi Sambo (now the Vice President of Nigeria), the late governor was the Chairman of the Textile Revival Committee which led to unprecedented state policy initiatives on the revival of the industry. As a governor of Kaduna State he together with the Vice President helped to reopen the hitherto closed UNTL plc in Kaduna which has commendably re-engaged over 1500 workers. Notwithstanding the serial security challenges in the state, Gov Yakowa never betrayed emotions or wavered. On the contrary, he remained to the last committed to the peace and industrial development of the State and ended as a true statesman and patriot. A perfect gentleman, Yakowa would be credited with harmony and peace. He was never crisis excited. Indeed he was crisis shy and crisis disillusioned at this hour we can only commiserate with the family of the late governor in particular, the government and good people of Kaduna State on this irreparable loss. May his soul rest in peace. May Allah forgive his sins and give us all the fortitude to bear the irreparable loss.

May his successor consolidate on his peace building efforts and sustain his pan-Nigerian vision of inclusion, and prosperity for all.

Essential Oshiomhole at 60*

On Thursday 4th of April 2013 two-term globally acclaimed former President of Nigeria Labour Congress (NLC) and Comrade Governor of Edo state, Adams Oshiomhole marks his 60th birthday anniversary. At its maiden Merit Award edition recently in Lagos, the Labour Writers Association of Nigeria (LAWAN), among others honoured the Comrade Governor for being a 'Pride of Modern Trade Unionism.' It was instructive that Labour writers singled out a second-term governor for a Pride of Modern Unionism merit award. Indeed the significant part of the citation on the comrade Governor was devoted to his almost four decades-long trade union carrier (1971-2007). Undoubtedly one essential and perhaps most critical attributes of Adams Oshiomhole is trade unionism. LAWAN certainly got it right; Life and times of comrade Adams show that his main strenuous preoccupations have been with the improvement in the working and living conditions of the working men and women. Not surprising that Adams the unionist, advocate, negotiator, the striker and mass organizer any day captures public imagination rather than Oshiomhole, twice democratically elected Governor, (the latest in which won in all the eighteen local governments, being the land-mark 18/18), the statesman, the humorist, peace-maker, pace-setter, the dancer, friend, father and grandfather.

A decade well before Comrade Adams started his working carrier in Arewa Textile mill in Kaduna in1971, Nelson Mandela (precisely in 1961!) had said 'Struggle is my life'. Looking at the well documented activities of the Labour leader in the last four decades one can conveniently conclude that 'Struggle is his (Adams') life'.

---

* *Daily Trust*, 1st April, 2013

As someone who succeeds him as the General Secretary of the National Union of Textile and Garment Workers' Union of Nigeria (NUTGWN), I bear witness that thousands of national and local collective agreements on wages, allowances, gratuities, hours of work, etc bear the bold signature imprint of Comrade Adams Oshiomhole in the textile industry. The union years of Adams were in a developmentist industrializing Nigeria. In the 1970s and 1980s, in Kaduna town alone, there were over ten large integrated textile mills that employed on the average 2,500 workers. United Textile Nigeria alone employed about 5000 workers. Indeed nationally there were as many as 200 textile mills with as many as 150,000 workers. Textile industry was the largest employer of labour followed by government. The labour market challenge was not unemployment but ensuring the work was decent in terms of pay, hours of work and security of work. This was where Comrade Adams and his colleagues audaciously made a difference, checked the authoritarian labour regimes of mainly Asian employers from China and India. It was the record achievements in textile union that eminently qualified Adams to become the 4th President of NLC where his impact was more felt in areas of improving on minimum wage, resisting persistent fuel price increases and struggling against casualization of labour force.

A look at the issues that preoccupied Adams and his comrades within the trade union movement show that what labour unions do are as all-inclusive as they are diverse; wage increase, decent jobs (anti-Casualisation) to watch other critical issues of societal significance as petroleum pricing and deregulation, privatisation, education (ASUU/Government conflicts), democracy (electoral bill, probity among politicians), anti-corruption, nationalism (Bakkassi), national unity, organizational building and capacity building, push for public welfare, good governance and democracy, liberation of Africa from poverty and underdevelopment and ignorance.

Under Oshiomhole union work took diverse forms, including advocacy, negotiation, mediation, mass-protests and, of course, strike action. What was clear was that all these forms of struggle were knowledge-driven. Indeed it was the quality of knowledge that Adams brought into the struggle that marked him out among other

NLC leaders after Hassan Sunmonu and Ali Chiroma, being the first and second Presidents of NLC respectively.

Interestingly, comrade Adams the unionist was not politically partisan. Indeed compared to unionists like Frank Kokori of NUPENG and Pascal Bafyau late former President of NLC, comrade Adams was politically shy as it were. He held the strong view that trade unions needed not be partisan for them to make independent case for the workers. Today it is a great paradox that Comrade Adams remains the most successful politically exposed trade unionists, winning two elections including land mark judgment that validated his first victory.

As Edo State Governor, even his political opponents bear witness to his unprecedented transformation in primary healthcare facilities and the building of new hospitals across the three senatorial districts and the 18 local governments.

Similar mileage is recorded in drastic improvement in education infrastructure – renovation of public schools, provision of learning aids and instruction materials, adequate deployment of teachers, model schools. Rural electrification and road construction have witnessed dramatic improvement under your leadership. He has also improved on job creation first through public works in which thousands of youths were employed and secondly through industrial development as witnessed by the recent monumental investment of over $2billion by Alhaji Aliko Dangote in the fertilizer plant at Agenebode. Adams has shown that comrades could be effective state actors just as well as they are effective non- state actors.

Significantly the comrade Governor has also shown that being in public office does not necessarily change one's loud advocacy for good governance. Adams has been as much loud in demanding for accountability and transparency in governance just as when he was a about leader. I recall that as a guest speaker at the Daily Trust annual dialogue in 2010 Comrade governor was the same vintage Discussant interrogating the assumptions of neo- liberalism ,insisting that contrary to the received wisdom, government has business in business and that governance cannot and should not be left to Market forces. Essential Oshimhole is committed to what you believe in. Happy birthday in advance comrade governor!

Olaitan Oyerinde: A Life Too Short*

Its a year we received with great shock the sad news of the assassination of the former Principal Private Secretary to the Edo State Governor, Comrade Adams Oshiomhole at his residence in Benin City during the early hours of Friday May 4th, 2012 by unknown assailants. This sad development came barely one week after the seeming orchestrated attack on the convoy of Comrade Governor Adams Oshiomhole that claimed the lives of three journalists and left several others injured. The cowardly murder of Comrade Olaitan is not only a great loss to the current administration of Comrade Adams Oshiomhole and the good people of Edo State that he diligently served for almost four years, but also to all of us in the labour movement. He was until his death also the Deputy General Secretary of the Nigeria Labour Congress (NLC) on leave of absence to Edo State. Comrade Olaitan as he was popularly called was a tested Comrade. I bear testimony to his hardwork, dedication and intellectual contribution to the growth and development of the Congress. He was among the first political appointees made by the Comrade Governor of Edo State shortly after his assumption of office as Governor of Edo State. Even as the Principal Private Secretary to Edo State Governor, Comrade Adams Oshiomhole, Comrade Olaitan effectively and commendably combined his duties with his responsibility in the Nigeria Labour Congress (NLC).

Textile Workers' Union bears the burden of the vacuum created by the dastardly murder of a worthy Comrade. His last support and solidarity for our union was during our last Delegates' Conference held in Asaba in March 2012. His singular intervention to

---

* *Daily Trust*, 6th May, 2013

ensure our tailor-members in Edo in their thousands attend the historic conference without stress underscored his allegiance to the labour movement. Few comrades look back when they have opportunity to be in government.

Like most progressive activists, he was truly a global citizen! Comrade Olaitain hailed from Osun State but many would readily insist he came from Kwara state where he had his primary, secondary and in part tiertery education. Indeed his lovely father and mother reside in Ilorin. His acceptance of an appointment as a Principal Private Secretary of the governor of Edo State and his posthumous celeberation as a hero of that state further attested to his pan Nigerian vision. His death came exactly when his services and energy were most needed in the great task of Edo State governance.

Its time all Nigerians rally around the government and good people of Edo State to unearth the murderers and get them prosecuted. At 44, Olaitan was one life too brutally cut short! Nigeria's unresolved individual murder cases (high or low) could very well lead to gradual decimation of a nation without an official declaration of war. Since Olatain's death last year, sixty lives of Nigerians were reportedly cut short in an open cattle market in Potiskum, Yobe state. Just recently no fewer than 185 people were killed during a clash between the militant Islamic sect, Boko Haram and the Multinational Joint Task Force in Baga, Borno State. We have inadvertently dignified unauthorised killings and reduced human lives and relations to mere statistics; "only 39"! When, indeed, killing a soul unjustly amounts to killing a humankind, so we are told in the Holy Book. Some historic murders, just like Olaitan, were not just statistics. They were well known names: Dele Giwa, Bola Ige, Engineer Funso Williams, Pa Alfred Rewane, Chiefs Dikibo, Harry Marshal, Suliat Adedeji, among other many lives cut too short. It is an open knowledge that Nigeria's life expectancy has sadly fallen bellow 50 years, no thanks to malaria, typhoid, cancers and scores of aviodable diseases associated with underdevelopment. With increasing cases of unresolved murder cases and mass killings in the land are we saying Nigerians should give up on life expentancy and be contended with death expectancy? A year after Olaitan's death, who cut a life so short and why?

Mandela is Dead, Long Live Madiba's Legacy![*]

"Fighters never say good bye," so declared in 1986 by Gracia Machel, in a dedication to her husband, Samora Machel then President of Mozambique whose plane was brutally shot down by the then cowardly racist South Africa. Life had it that Gracia Machel would again become a widow to Nelson Mandela, the best of humanity in twenty-first century.

Last Thursday 5th of December, 2013 the world received with heavy heart the eventual departure of Nelson Mandela the founding father of modern democratic South Africa and a towering political figure out of Africa in the 21st century.

His death was a shock coming just few months after the good people of the world with remarkable gratitude marked his 95th birthday despite his old age/health related challenge. Fighters certainly never say good bye. In recent months, following his last health challenge, many admirers had thought he would depart earlier. But Madiba left at a time most camera men had departed his home following his recovery. Although for those that cared, Mandela as far back as 2011 had said "am not sick, I am old." We join the progressive humankind to mourn his death.

The departure of a freedom fighter, global icon for forgiveness and unprecedented transition from tyranny to non-racial democracy is capable of ushering a global despair, disillusionment and agony. As a unionist, I bear witness that Madiba was a close ally of the global trade union movement both in the struggle against Apartheid and

[*] *Daily Trust*, Monday December 9, 2013

decent work agenda as demanded by the International Labour Organisation (ILO). According to Mandela, "job, jobs and jobs are the dividing line in many families between a decent life and a wretched existence." By this statement Nelson Mandela rightly pointed out that life is miserable without work. Madiba was fully at home with trade unions and trade unionists alike. Indeed the Republic of South Africa runs on the tripod of the ruling political party, ANC, Council of South Afrcican Trade Unions, COSATU and the South African Communist Party.

Today, there is undoubtedly a Nelson Mandela vacuum in the world turned asunder by widening gap between the poor and the rich, avoidable violence and wars of attrition, injustices of varying types, vengeance and non-forgiveness.

However, the world must take consolation on the fact that immortality was certainly not the way of Nelson Mandela. Immortality belongs to Almighty God! What should hunt humanity like spectre are Mandela's deeds. Let's celebrate and emulate his life of amazing sacrifices with dignity, brief and remarkable tenure in office, forgiveness and reconciliation and value addition in retirement.

We are right to legitimately agonize over the inevitable death of the beloved Madiba. But after agonizing we must rise up like Mandela to organize for a better world, freedom and liberty. Like Mandela, let us dedicate ourselves to the struggle of the humanity, cherish "the ideal of a democratic and free society in which all persons live together in harmony and with equal opportunities."

Annual UN Mandela Day on July 18th which is also Mandela's birthday offers us opportunity to further inspire individuals and nations to take action to help change the world for the better, and in doing so build a global movement for public good.

Mandela was the President of South Africa from 1994 to 1999. He was however less remembered for the presidency where he commendably exercised power to protect the weak and the minority without necessarily demonizing the strong and privileged. His enduring legacy was his unique ability to exercise power to forgive those who jailed him for twenty-seven years. He was a true symbol of reconciliation in the world polarized along ethnic, racial and class cleavages and in a world bleeding under scores of false leaders.

Thanks to Mandela brand, Africa for once hosted the 2010 FIFA soccer world cup. That year Mandela brand linked all the polarities in South Africa and indeed in the world together and reminded each of the contending elements of the virtues of sacrifice, forgiveness and reconciliation. The critical question is; who leads again like Madiba? May God make his grave more spacious and comfortable more than the vast world he positively impacted upon.

Nelson Mandela, the day After*

There is no doubt about it. More than any other historic figure, Nelson Mandela could be said to have determined the character and the outlook of the new non-racial democratic South Africa. Judging by the rainbow of outpours of tributes, he almost came out as a 'Saint Mandela' in a world suffering from the crisis of leadership at various levels. Interestingly he was once likened to a Saint, albeit in a mischievous manner by no less a person than President Robert Mugabe of Zimbabwe. In a documentary in May this year, Mugabe was reported to have said Mandela went "a bit too far in doing good to the non-black communities, really in some cases at the expense of (blacks)." "That's being too saintly, too good, too much of a saint," he said. A day after the historic burial of Nelson Mandela's remains at his beloved rural childhood village of Qunu the point must be made that the 95-year old historic figure was no 'Nietzschean Superman' or 'demiurge of history'. He actually had a disdain for hero-worship and sycophancy of various hues. "I have always been unhappy about my depiction as a demi-god" Mandela once said. I agree with his life long friend and a Nobel Peace Laureate, Desmond Tutu that as great as he was, Nelson Mandela was "...only one pebble on the beach, one of thousands". "Not an insignificant pebble, I' II grant you that, but a pebble all the same" he added.

To appreciate Mandela we must not forget to appreciate thousands of other comrades who together with him selflessly put their lives on the line for liberty and freedom. We cannot forget, Walter Sisulu, Givan Mbeki, Oliver Thambo, scores of visible and invincible Robben Island prisoners. I visited Robben notorious

* *ThisDay*, Monday December 16, 2013

Island in 2001 as a tourist. I bear witness that there were thousands of Mandelas who gave all they had to ensure a free and democratic South Africa. Lest we forget Nelson Mandela himself deliberately shared the credit of leadership with others. The present day Nigerian syndrome of a single leader or god-father is alien to Mandela. He was once asked about his reaction to the compilation of a CD of his collected greatest speeches on a SABC (South African Broadcasting Corporation) morning live programme. His response was worth being read; "Vuyo (the TV presenter) I feel bad because the CD does not give a fair picture of this country's history. You and I know that the greatest of speakers among the men and women that waged the struggle against Apartheid I am not even eloquent". "I would have been happier if my speeches were simply some among the great speeches that were made by our country's eminent personalities such as Oliver Tambo, Chris Hani, Walter Sisulu, among many others. By so doing, we would be painting the right picture of our country's history...the reality of our struggle is that no individual among us can claim to have played a great role from the rest." Mandela's response is recommended for the likes of former President Olusegun Obasanjo and eternally sit-tight President Robert Mugabe about how not to assume that only they and they alone deserve the honour of nations they preside over often for the worse.

A visitor from the outer space reading most of the tributes on Mandela would rightly have an impression that the great icon was "self- made" in the sense of the rat race of the world of greed and self accumulation. It is certainly easier and convenient to take the pictures of Mandela as an amateur boxer, a prisoner and a president of a Republic (almost in-that-order). But the history of struggle (which undoubtedly was his life) for freedom and eventual triumph is far more complex than the global media presented it. Nelson Mandela was a product of historic reality as much as Gandhi was in India, Kwame Nkrumah was in Ghana, Nnamdi Azikiwe was in Nigeria and George Washington was in USA. To this extent, there will always be more Mandelas if the historic conditions dictate. Significantly too, Nelson Mandela was a product of an organisation, namely African National Congress (ANC). The ANC was formed in 1912, six years well before Mandela was born. He undoubtedly together with others radicalised the ANC in the 1950s and 1960s from mere appeal to oppressors to open confrontation with the regime of Apartheid. He nonetheless did this within the context of an organisation. The core principles of ANC are pan-Africanism, socialism and even communism. Nelson Mandela once said: "I am a member of the ANC. I have been a member of ANC and I will remain a member until I die." Mandela's staying power in an organisation that was once legalised, once banned and later unbanned spanning over a century contrasts sharply with the current carpet crossing of Nigeria"s modern day politicians. Lest we forget, no short cut to freedom and certainly without building institutions especially political parties with clear cut ideologies we can hardly build a sustainable democratic society.

I read through the great tribute of President Barack Obama at Mandela memorial. Many thanks to Obama for reminding us of Madiba's 1964 trail speech where he said:

> "I have fought against white domination and I have fought against black domination." Obama also commendably observed that there are "...too many of us who happily embrace Madiba's legacy of racial reconciliation, but passionately resist even modest reforms that would challenge chronic poverty and growing inequality. There are too many leaders who claim solidarity with Madiba's struggle for freedom, but do not tolerate dissent from their own people. And there are too many of us who stand on the sidelines, comfortable in complacency or cynicism when our voices must be heard."

Well put! But Obama did not go far enough to point out that United States of America under Ronald Regan and Britain under Margret Thatcher actually stood on the sidelines and indeed collaborated with Apartheid regime while Mandela and others were unjustly imprisoned. Lest we forget that the battle against Apartheid was won with American and British people but certainly not with their governments who did dirty business with Apartheid. By the way lest we forget where was Nigeria's voice at Mandela memorial? Lest we forget; Nigeria was once a frontline state in the struggle against Apartheid just as Tanzania and Cuba.

Alao-Aka Bashorun: Pan African to the core*

Tomorrow Tuesday, 7th of January in Lagos, Babatunde Raji Fashola, SAN the thirteenth governor of Lagos State unveils a worthy bust and a public park dedicated to the former President of Nigeria Bar Association (NBA), late Alao Aka Bashorun. Alao Aka-Bashorun was the thirteenth elected President of NBA from year 1987 to 1989. He died in 2005. When his remains was laid to rest in 2005, yours sincerely wrote in tribute to my mentor and senior comrade, that "If there should be a worthy epitaph that captures inestimable national value additions of the late legendary activist progressive lawyer it should read: "A Patriot to the core". Patriotism in Nigeria was then (and is certainly still) out of fashion. No thanks to the elitist slide back to regionalism, parochialism, corruption, narrow-mindedness, and shameless chauvinism. Few endangered species called patriots fully appreciated the significance of Aka's patriotism and how Nigeria then just lost a voice after the death of the great patriot Dr Bala Usman of Ahmadu Bello University Zaria, also a comrade of Aka Bashorun. Many thanks to the government and people of Lagos State for the deserved posthumous dedication in honour of an African patriot, a revolutionary and a radical lawyer. In him was a great human capital. Late Alao Aka-Bashorun was a law graduate from the prestigious London School of Economics where he did his LL.B Programme in 1957 with schoolmates like legal luminary and elder statesman, Professor Ben Nwabueze (SAN). Alao Aka-Bashorun was born on December 5, 1930 to a Lagos Island family. The

* *Daily Trust*, Monday January 6, 2014

posthumous honour to the late NBA President and radical progressive lawyer is coming up after the death and burial of Nelson Mandela, the first democratically elected non-racial President of South Africa. Remembering Aka today invokes among others a nostalgia of his impeccable pan African credentials that compare favourably with Madiba's in terms of selflessness, courage, perseverance and passion for liberty, fairness and justice. Indeed Nigeria once produced many Mandelas that included Aka Bashorun. As an undergraduate he was an activist and once elected the President of the West African Students Union (WASU) in 1957. He was on the barricade together with other patriotic first generation Nigerian students in the 1960s denouncing Anglo-Nigeria defence pact in the knowledge that the promise of independence was not neo-colonialism. He was also a union organiser at the then United African Company (UAC) headquarters in Lagos where he worked. With inspirations from great pan African leaders like Dr. Kwame Nkrumah the President of Ghana, Dr. Sekou Toure of Guinea and Dr. Felix Mourne of Cameroon and other progressive nationalist politicians Aka for decades engaged in full time revolutionary activities. An organizational man, he had to his credit many progressive pan African organizations whose objectives included fighting for equality and justice to all. He was one of the activists that canvassed for the formation of Nigeria Labour Congress in 1978. Aka successfully organized the first anti-Apartheid meeting in the United Kingdom in 1960. He was an unofficial Senior Advocate of Nigeria dating back to colonial era. Paradoxically he was not so honoured with official SAN by the law bureaucracy before his death. In fact, the great irony is that those so generously privileged as official advocates of Nigeria are now in the habit of questioning the existence of Nigeria which the late Aka cherished until his death. Aka Bashorun raised the banner of democracy, rule of law and internationalism to the end. His remarkable reinvention of the hitherto moribund Bar, as the President of NBA, during the dark days of military dictatorship only increased the noise level of his strident advocacy for Nigeria. To protest the incessant disobedience of court orders by IBB military junta Aka organized the first national boycott of courts in 1988. He opposed in particular the notorious

Decree 2 and other obnoxious laws. Notwithstanding his radicalism, both the activists of left and right saw him as a consensus builder.

Aka Bashorun legal Chambers at Jebba West in Lagos was the Nigeria's equivalent of legendary Mandela-Oliver legal office at Fox Street, Johannesburg which opened doors to justice and fairness for the multitude of the oppressed and under privileged. Aka Bashorun was a meticulous lawyer who shared traditions with famous progressive lawyers who put law at the service of the oppressed such as South Africa's late Yusuf Dadoo, Alfred Nzo, Nelson Mandela and Oliver Tambo. Aka Chambers was also a remarkable platform for national integration. Not few lawyers have passed through the chambers that included Bob Manuel, Femi Falana, Tony Akika among others. Aka Bashorun will ever be remembered for his comradeship and generosity. Socialism was not for him a slogan of convenience or passing fad to seek relevance and prominence but a means for practical deeds to lift those lagging behind in the rat race of life under capitalism. Yours truly, late Dr Bala Muhammed and Chom Bagu Deme were direct beneficiaries of his generosity and solidarity. He single-handedly handled our case against Ango Abdullahi inspired repressive mass expulsion of 1981 in ABU Zaria. My indebtedness even borders on romanticism precisely because I own my first air travel to him in the 1980s. A remarkable elegant and successive advocate, Aka Bashorun was conscious of the limitations of law as tool for transformation. He told us that we could only get judgment and not necessarily justice in the court during our battle against expulsion. He accordingly advised that we return back to school even if it entailed starting afresh adding that nothing was too much (including time) in search for knowledge. Today we dedicate our multiple degrees and certificates own heap to Aka Bashorun's worthy counseling. Aka's well having and well giving was done in obscurity as part of his modesty. May his soul rest in peace.

Tribute to Comrade Aloysius Morgan Anigbo *mni*

"Fighters never say good bye"; Gracia Machel, widow of Samora Machel and Nelson Mandela'

The remains of Comrade Aloysius Morgan Anigbo, mni was laid to eternal rest last Friday, 9th of May at his country home of Amankwo-Eko, Enugu state. Yours comradely was among the numerous immediate and extended family members, well wishers and comrades of the late Morgan to bid a worthy fighter an eternal farewell. I was there as a comrade and family friend of the diseased, representative of NLC President, Comrade Abdulwaheed Omar and representative of the President of Alumni Association of the National Institute, (AANI) both of which Comrade Aloysius Morgan was a proud member underscoring his value addition as an organizational man. May his soul rest in perfect peace.

Like many other well meaning Nigerians, the sad news of the death of Comrade Aloysius Morgan Anigbo, mni came to us with a great shock. He passed away on Wednesday 26th February 2014 at University of Nigeria Teaching Hospital, Enugu, during a brief illness, at the age of 81.

He was a pioneer Head of Organisation of the Nigeria Labour Congress (NLC) after the historic restructuring of the NLC by Murtala/Obasanjo military regime in 1978. His dedication to organising made him to be popularly nicknamed 'ORGANIZED'. Appreciating the primacy of Organizing to the labour movement, Comrade Anigbo was a tested foot soldier of African working class. Interestingly, he started his working career as a reporter and proof reader with *The Daily Comet*, one of Late Dr. Nnamdi Azikiwe' newspapers. He was a militant Zikist during the historic struggle for

Nigerian Independence in the 1940s and 1950s! He was a member of Staff Consultative Council of UAC, Northern District Headquarters before serving as the National Organising Secretary of Electrical Workers Union of Nigeria and the Camerouns.

He was appointed General Secretary of Railway Technical Staff Association from where he went to study Industrial Relations at Xavier Institute of Industrial and Labour Relations, and Cornell University in New York. He was at various times a National Treasurer of the Nigerian Union of Railwaymen Federated. He was a Co-ordinating Secretary of Nigerian Affiliated Trade Unions to the International Transport Workers Federation. At the Nigeria Labour Congress (NLC), he rose from the rank of Pioneer Head of Organisation of the Congress in 1978 to become Deputy General Secretary. He retired as Acting General Secretary of NLC after the unfortunate intervention of the Abacha regime in the affairs of the NLC in 1994. Comrade Anigbo was part of the great struggles of NLC for minimum wage in 1981, 1992 and decent work in general under three NLC Presidents, namely Comrades Alhaji Hassan Sunmonu, Ali Chiroma, mni, late Pascal Bafyau, mni.

Late Comrade Anigbo, mni was an active alumnus of the National Institute of Policy and Strategic Studies (NIPSS) Kuru, Jos. He was a participant of Senior Executive Course (SEC) 13/1991. Late Comrade Anigbo, mni was one of the foremost trade union leaders that successfully attended the National Institute of Policy and Strategic Studies (NIPSS) in addition to other courses and conferences at home and abroad. His study on the role of Nigerian trade unions in national development has remained a useful reference material to many researchers till date. As an active member of the Alumni Association of the National Institute, (AANI), late Comrade Anigbo participated in most activities of the Association including our Annual General Meetings (AGMs) for a better society.

We join millions of people to give testimony that Late Comrade Aloysius Anigbo, mni was a tested Comrade. We bear witness to his tremendous contributions to the growth and development of the Nigeria Labour Congress (NLC) in particular and the Nigeria labour movement in general. He was highly dedicated and committed to the defence of workers rights, trade unions unity and working class solidarity.

Late Comrade Anigbo was a global citizen and participated in a number of courses and conferences at home and abroad. He was multi-skilled as a working reporter and organiser in various unions that included electricity and railways unions. He was at varying times both an elected and appointed labour leader in the cause of serving the working people of Nigeria and Africa. He was part of the great success stories of Nigerian working people for the right to organise and free collective bargain for minimum wage, fair working hours and income adequacy after work (pension).

His death is a great loss to his family, the Alumni Association of the National Institute and the global labour movement he diligently served for many years. At a time our country increasingly loses committed patriots, Nigeria will definitely miss the singular passion, patriotism and commitment of Comrade Morgan Anigbo. The late Nelson Mandela once rightly observed about life that; "What counts in life is not the mere fact that we have lived. It is what difference we have made to lives of others that will determine the significance of the life we lead." Undoubtedly Comrade Anigbo lived a rewarding life that has made positive difference to the lives of African working people in terms of dignity of labour, adequate pay among others.

May the Almighty God grant him eternal rest.

Dora Akunyili: tribute to a worthy regulator*

Last Saturday, the former Anambra State Governor, Peter Obi, formally announced the death of Professor Dora Nkem Akunyili erstwhile Director General of the National Agency for Food and Drugs Administration and Control (NAFDAC). She reportedly died of a poorly diagnosed protracted cancer, a paradoxical health story for a public officer with knack for details that saved many Nigerian lives.

Professor Dora was also a former Minister of Information and Communication and a delegate to the on-going National Conference. She was even a contestant to the Senate. The first class scholar and multiple award-winner for work in pharmacology, public health and human rights was born in Makurdi, Benue State, on July 14, 1954 though hailed from Nanka, Anambra State.

Her profile can certainly fill many pages. But above all Dora would be better remembered as a successful regulator of the country's drug and food market. She courageously "took on the hydra-headed problem of fake, spurious, unwholesome and substandard drugs, turning fortunes around for the nation's lopsided drug distribution system and quickly gaining international recognition as a true advocate for public health and human rights protection". John Ralston Saul, the Canadian author once noted that"…regulation protects the marketplace from itself by introducing commonsense. In the process, it protects society". Never before had a singular regulatory agency's campaign for standard and quality added such

* Monday June 9th, 2014

value of unprecedented proportions in pharmaceutical sectors like NAFDAC did under Dora Akunyili.

In the standard cliché of neo- liberal reform-agenda, we are made to belief that: private sector is the engine of growth. Dora's NAFDAC showed that while private sector could be the engine, public sector indeed oiled this engine through vigilance and standard enforcement, without which the former crashes into smithereens. The remarkable recovery of drugs and food manufacturing sector from near zero capacity to full production on accounts of NAFDAC's keeping faith with its mandate of enforcing standard under Dora leadership must serve as a reference point for other sectors and other public agencies. NAFDAC under Dora showed that domestic commonsense and passion to enforce the rules promoted win-win outcomes of safety and job-creation compared to uncritical received wisdom of market forces , which fuels zero-sum game of profit for few drug merchants, poverty and death for many innocent others. Put in another way, our salvation lies in our resolve to look at the faces of our people (here, consumers of drugs) and local producers (here, drug manufacturers) through standardization. Dora's seven-year tenure at NAFDAC shows that the intellectual/doctrinaire assault on public institutions as inefficient, corrupt presented by IMF and World Bank (paradoxically these are also global super public institutions) is unhelpful and should be ignored. NAFDAC shows that public agencies can work like any other private agency when knowledge-driven. Dora's impeccable credentials and her passion to overcome the Nigerian malaise of sickening disconnect between knowledge and performance or the appalling connect between knowledge and dishonesty and corruption explains her remarkable achievements. According to her, before she took over NAFDAC, we "had a regulatory agency for over two decades and it was as if we have no regulatory agency". "We had counterfeit drugs, drugs without active ingredients, drugs with insufficient active ingredients, drugs that were labelled what they were not, and, of course, expired drugs." How many chieftains of our existing hundreds of parastatals and regulatory agencies can look at the past with such disdain on accounts of making an appreciative change?

Akunyili was certainly not *tokunbo.* She was not out sourced from Diaspora either. She was home-grown. It was even self-evident that she was monthly paid in naira. Dora herself attributed her success to the support by all, namely from President she served to her workforce and millions of anonymous praying Nigerians. The lesson here is that motivation for public officers needs not necessarily be dollarized but could flow from the support and solidarity of the employer and above all, the conviction, productivity and dedication of the public officer to his/her calling and humanity in general. The challenge however is the sustainability of NAFDAC model of regulation. Whatever NAFDAC is today, Dora's tenure remains a reference point of performance. Understandably her numerous outstanding awards can fill a library. They included "the Time Magazine Award 2006 (One of the 18 Heroes of our Time) – Time, Inc.; Person of the Year 2005 Award by Silverbird Communications Ltd; Award of Excellence by Integrated World Services (IWS), Dec. 2005; Award of Excellence - Advocacy for Democracy Dividends International, Lagos; Meritorious Award 2005; An Icon of Excellence Award by the African Cultural Institute and Zenith Bank Plc; 2005 Grassroots Human Rights Campaigner Award London Based Human Rights Defence Organization, 2005; Most Innovative Director Award Federal Government College, Ijanikin, Lagos, 2005 and Integrity Award 2003 winner given by Transparency International. May her soul rest in perfect peace.

Olaitan Oyerinde: Blessed Are the Dead*

Last Saturday 28th of June 2014, a book entitled; OLAITAN *Oyerinde: His Struggles For A Better Nigeria* was formally presented to the public at Comrade Olaitan Oyerinde Hall, Labour House Abuja commendably named after him by NLC leadership. The occasion paraded progressive dignitaries that included President, Nigeria Labour Congress (NLC), Comrade Abdulwahed Omar, the Honourable Commissioner, Establishment, Edo State, Comrade Didi Adodo who was also the Book Presenter and Special Guest of Honour, Mr. Labaran Maku, Honourable Minister of Information and the wife of Late Comrade Olaitan Oyerinde, Mrs. Funke Oyerinde, NAC members of Nigeria Labour Congress (NLC) and Presidents and General Secretaries of Industrial Unions.

The author is Lois Otse Adams. The 256-page book of some over 50,000 healing word-count chronicles the struggles of Comrade Olaitan, former Principal Private Secretary to Edo State Governor, Comrade Adams Oshiomhole. Yours comradely, was the book reviewer, as directed and encouraged by the President of NLC, Abdulwaheed Omar. Late Olaitan Aremu Oyerinde was a comrade and friend to many of us. Undoubtedly he was a special son to his parents, namely Mr. Azeez Oyerinde his father, a veteran Journalist and Mrs. Comfort Oyerinde, a trader. He was also an acknowledged possessive brother to his lovely siblings. The great contribution of the author, Louis Otse Adams lies in her ability to weave together the varying positive attributes of Comrade Olaitan to give us a complete picture of a patriot, a revolutionary, a tested unionist, an organizer, a loyal worker, a mentor and a proud father of three and husband. On

* Monday June 30th, 2014

May 4, 2012 Comrade Olaitan then a Principal Private Secretary to Edo State Governor, Comrade Adams Oshiomhole around midnight was brutally murdered at his residence in Benin, before family members. His cowardly murder had added to the increasing cases of unresolved killings of politically exposed individuals in Nigeria, well documented mystery deaths by the author in Chapter Five; End Of A Dream. Olaitan's murder raises the painful memory of the unresolved deaths of political notables like Bola Ige, Pa Alfred Rewane, Dele Giwa, Chief Marshall Harry, Engr Funsho Williams among others.

We are still saddled with the embarrassing conflicting accounts and outcomes of separate investigations by the Nigerian Police and the Department of State Security (DSS) since 2012, on Olaitan's killers. But while we are weighed down with the mystery of his death, Lois Otse lifted our spirit in a compelling essay about the struggles of Comrade Olaitan and his contributions to humanity spanning over two decades out of his relatively short 44 years in life.

In this book we get raw evidences of a patriot and global citizen almost from cradle to grave. He was "was born in Ilorin on the pleasant day of December 7, 1968" to a mother from Ilesha in Osun State and a father who though from Ede in Osun state adapted Ilorin, Kwara state as a home. Comrade Olaitain's parents hailed from Osun State but many would readily insist he came from Kwara State where he had his primary, secondary and in part tertiary education. He schooled in Lagos and worked in Abuja and with union work almost all parts of Nigeria and indeed the world. As a student activist, he had known all parts of the country well before he graduated. Serving the nation through the compulsory NYSC was just an official legitimization of his earned national outlook. His acceptance of an appointment as a Principal Private Secretary of the governor of Edo State and his post humous celebration as a hero of Edo state; and indeed Nigeria as a whole further attested to his pan Nigerian vision. A revised edition must bring to bear Comrade Olaitain's international work as the head of NLC international department showing that he was indeed an internationalist callously denied us by the murderers. Olaitan was a brand-name in Johannesburg, Berlin, Geneva, Ghana and Togo, Kenya where he had added value to the struggle of the working people of the world.

Chapter 4 (pages 49 to 78) gives us the photo album of the life and times of Olaitan. Baby Olaitan looked as confident as comrade father Olaitan and interestingly Left-leaning of the camera as a baby, a riddle that has been solved by Olaitan's left-leaning progressive calling in life. But the bigger picture lies in his positive sayings and writings for a better Nigeria as contained in this book. The quotable Olaitan in this book is about bigger positive picture of Nigeria. In a country in which millions of youths are being recruited into ethnic and religious bigotry, Olaitan through this book is a worthy model patriot.

Olaitan also came out as a loyal organizational man who lived on dignity of labour, not theft or corruption. Some of the organizations to his credit included Thomas Sankara Movement (TSM), Youth Solidarity on Southern Africa (YUSSA), Patriotic Youth Movement of Nigeria (PYMN), the University of Lagos Students' Union and the National Association of Nigerian Students (NANS), Iron and Steel Senior Staff Association of Nigeria (ISSSAN) and the Senior Staff Consultative Association of Nigeria (SSCAN) and Nigeria Labour Congress (NLC). In a country in which scores of registered political parties lack clear-cut ideological orientation, this book fires our imagination about formations of ideologically motivated organizations to advance the struggle for better Africa.

The author also shows that contrary to the false impression that comrades and progressive are motivated by depreciations, Olaitan's example shows that those who often fight for better society are only angry about underdevelopment not hungry for materialism. In terms of class as a son of a working journalist in the 1960s, he shared the same background with the likes of Nelson Mandela, Frantz Fanon who consciously chose to fight for the mass of the oppressed rather than pursuing material selfish interests. In the book we also see Comrade Olaitan as "...a bundle of humour". According to her, "he had this uncanny way of cracking rib-cracking jokes and yet kept a straight face while others would laugh to stupor." To those who, for instance, wanted to see him as an outsider in Edo government calling him "Mr. Expatriate" (he hailed from Osun), he returned with a joke instead of hard feelings; "But you people are not paying me expatriate wage unlike my contemporaries from overseas." "If you got angry with him, he would disarm you with jokes." May his soul rest in peace.

Dr. Jibrin Ibrahim at sixty - not by politics alone*

"Age is a question of mind over matter. If you don't mind it doesn't matter" - Dan Ingrams

I missed the merriment on Sunday, 29th of November, the 60th birthday of Dr. Jibrin Ibrahim which I gathered paraded notable friends like Professor Attahiru Jega, Chairman, Independent National Electoral Commission (INEC), Mr Dapo Olorunyomi, editor in chief Premium times, Mr Danlami Nmodu, publisher/editor in chief Newsdiaryonline.com, Dr Kole Shettima, Comrade John Odah former General Secretary, Nigeria Labour Congress (NLC) and Professor Abubakar Momoh among other civil society activists. However I was at the intellectual manifestation of the 1st of December Monday evening, at the Yar'Adua Centre, Abuja that paraded great human capital that included former Chief Justice of the Federation, Justice Muhammed Uwais and his wife, Maryam, were present. Equally present were Professors Jega and Ibrahim Gambari, ex-minister, ex-Nigerian ambassador to the United Nations (etc.), Dr Abubakar Siddique, Mallam Kabiru Yusuf, chairman/CEO, Media Trust Ltd, Femi Falana, SAN, Comrade Odah, yours comradely (Issa Aremu and my wife, Hamdalat), Hadiza Bala Usman and her husband, my dear friend, Yakubu Tanimu, Ekanem Bassey and other civil society activists including YZ Yau, CDD director Idayat Hassan, Auwal Musa Rafsanjani of CISLAC, Samson Itodo, and Kunle Fagbemi among others.

---

* Monday December 8, 2014

Monday's event featured intellectual fireworks by a panel that included the celebrant, Dr Jibo, Professsor Adele Jinadu and Professor Okey Ibeano. Incidentally the three of them share the same birthday but certainly not by accident, they made up the panel which robustly interrogated the critical question; is political science in Nigeria dead, alive or in comatose? The moderator was Funmi Olanisekan of Kings College, Oxford, UK.

Those who spoke earlier in extolling the virtues of Dr. Jibo included Mrs. Uwais, co-chair, Jibo's wife, Dr Charmaine Pereira, Falana, SAN, YZ Yau, Hadiza, Odah, Chris Kwajah, Yunusa Tanko of IPAC and Professor Gambari. Of particular significance was the reminiscence by Professor Gambari who as a former teacher to Dr Jibo gave testimony about his track record of "humility, intellectual acuity, commitment to truth, principle and the struggle for a better Nigeria". There was a nostalgia about the old great Faculty of Arts and Social Sciences (FASS) of Ahmadu Bello University (ABU) Samaru Zaria from where Jibo studied, in early 1970s, graduated, taught in the 1980s and retired in 1990s. Many thanks to Professor Gambari who reminded us that there was once a Nigeria where universities were centres of principled discourse without personal animosities. Almost by accident (or was it by design?) the moderator, Funmi Olanisekan, of the evening session on political science in Nigeria dead, alive or in comatose in Nigeria denied me recognition. I had wanted to point out that our gathering that night underscored the fact that political science is alive in Nigeria. Where else can a 60th birthday be observed with such social-scientific star-words about the state, nation, government, politics and policies of government as we witnessed that historic night in honour of Dr Jibo? Where else can a celebrant be a discussant canvassing unorthodox view according to which political science was long dead when political scientists joined IBB political contraptions of the 1980s? Certainly political science was alive that night when, Dr Jibo, true to principled type, said it as he felt even with the presence of the co-panelist Professor Adele Jinadu, who was a notable in IBB political kitchen cabinet. But the most provocative was Professor Okey Ibeano whose intervention further shows that political science is alive in Nigeria. According to him, the challenge of today's Nigeria is how to bridge the widening gap between what he said to be politics of affluence and politics of affliction. His concluding suggestion was certainly reassuring; we must use the affluence of the few to cure the affliction of the majority poor failing which the affliction of the many poses danger to all. The life and times of Dr Jibo shows that it is possible that we promote commonwealth in place of personal aggrandizement. It is possible to promote well being of the majority without undermining the well- having and well deserving of the few. I recall the friendship and brotherhood Dr Jibo and Dr Rauf Mustapha extended to my young family in early 1980s. We were not as intellectually endowed then. But through their encouragement and support, me and late Dr Bala Muhammed completed our studies notwithstanding the short set backs inflicted by Ango Abdullahi dictatorship in ABU in early 1980s. The way Dr Jibo and his wife generously opened their doors to us taught the lesson in hospitality. Certainly Jibo's pedigree (a former Associate Professor at the Department of Political Science, Ahmadu Bello University, Zaria, Nigeria!) is intimidatingly political but the other Jibo is more than politics. He does exhibit comradeship, friendship and capacity to cook tasty fish pepper-soup and *isiewu*. Happy 60th birthday to Jibrin Ibrahim, a Senior Fellow at the Centre for Democracy & Development, a regional research, advocacy and training non-governmental organisation for West Africa.

Index

Abashi, Chris; 35, 36
Abdallah, Raji; 55
Abdullahi, Ango; 8, 71, 112, 115, 152
Abdulraheem, Dr Tajudeen; 49, 117-120, 125
Abiola, *Bashorun;* 22, 179
Abisoye, Major-General Emmanuel; 115
Abubakar, Atiku; 70, 91
Abubakar, Sidiq; 6
Academic Staff Union of Universities (ASUU); 9, 112, 115, 122
Achebe, Chinua; 40-42, 87, 89, 133
Adamu, Dr Haroun; 136
Adebayo, Cornelius; 23
Adebo, Simeon; 11-13
Adebola, Alhaji H.P; 11, 109
Adedoyin, Raheem; 21
Adjei, Arke; 73
Ajayi, Professor Ade; 55, 56
Ajuluchukwu, MCK; 32, 33
Akanbi, Justice Mustapha; 65, 86, 131-133
Akande, Chief Bisi ; 62
Ake, Claude; 5, 14-17, 38, 126, 170
Akika, Tony; 57, 203
Akinjide, Chief Richard; 53, 55
Akufo-Addo; 73
Akunyili, Dora; 207
Alagoa, E.J; 56
Albright, Madeleine; 20
Alemika, Professor Etannibi; 170
Aluko, Professor Sam; 174
Anenih, Chief Tony; 91
Anigbo, Comrade Aloysius Morgan; 204

Anikulapo-Kuti, Fela; 78-81, 126
Annan, Kofi; 73
Anyim, Anyim Pius; 161
Arafat, Yasser; 43-45
Attah, Adamu; 23
Awolowo, Chief Obafemi; 10, 23, 39, 89, 100, 129, 168, 185
Awoniyi, Sunday; 82-85
Azazi, General Andrew; 187
Azikiwe, Dr; 10, 39, 55, 84, 100, 168, 199
Aziz, Tariq; 20
Babangida, Ibrahim; 177
Bafyau, Comrade Pascal; 177-180, 192
Bagu, Chom; 35
Bala, Dr. Jubril; 34, 35
Balewa, Sir Abubakar Tafawa; 89, 141, 164
Bangura, Yusuf; 7
Barak, Ehud; 44
Bashorun, Alao Aka; 52, 55-57, 126, 201-203
Bassey, Ekanem; 214
Bassey, Etim; 12
Battuta, Muhammad Ibn Abdullahi; 39
Beckman, Bjorn; 7
Belgore, Justice Alfa Babatunde; 139
Bella, Ahmed Ben; 158
Bello, Sir Ahmadu; 55, 84, 89, 129, 168, 185
Biko, Steve; 38
Blair, Tony; 96, 98
Bongo, Omar; 145
Bush, George H. W.; 155
Bush, George W.; 96, 103, 108, 155
Cabral, Amilcal; 5, 14, 99, 126
Carter, Jimmy; 76, 77, 102, 121
Castro, Fidel; 1-4, 69, 126, 155, 157-160
Castro, Raul; 158
Chikerema, James; 97
Chiroma, Ali; 111, 114, 177-179, 192
Chitepo, Herbert; 97
Clinton, Bill; 20, 69, 76, 101, 104, 107, 108, 131, 181
Clinton, Hillary; 107
Cost of Living Allowance (COLA); 11

Dadoo, Yusuf; 203
Danfodio, Uthman; 39
Dangote, Alhaji Aliko; 192
Danjuma, Gen Theophilus; 162
Davidson, Basil; 49, 61
De Klerk, Fredrick; 69
Deme, Chom Bagu; 57, 203
Dikko, Lamis; 35
Doe, Samuel; 63
Durban UN Conference on Racism and Xenophobia; 19
Ejiofor SOZ; 179
Elias, I.O.; 12, 13
Ero-Philips, P.O.; 151
Essential Imoudu; 10-13
Essential Saraki; 21
Essential Shagari At 80; 28-30
Fagbemi, Kunle; 214
Falana, Femi; 57, 125, 184-186, 203, 214
Fani-Kayode, Femi; 40-42
Fanon, Frantz; 14, 49, 61, 126
Fasehun, Dr Frederick; 56
Fawehinmi, Gani; 38, 125-150, 129, 169
Fayemi, Dr Kayode; 161
Gaddafi, M; 62, 146
Gambari, Professor Ibrahim Agboola; 87-90, 132, 133, 164-166, 214
Gambo, Hajia; 169
Gandhi, Indira; 2, 126
Gandhi, Mahatma; 126, 199
Garvey, Marcus; 6
Gbadamosi, Chief Rasheed; 78
Giwa, Dele; 38, 211
Goodluck, Wahab ; 11, 12, 109
Gowon, Gen.; 154, 161, 169, 176
Grail, Roger; 11
Guevera, Che; 2, 126
Hani, Chris; 199
Hart, Armando; 159
Hashim, Yahaya; 179
Hassan, Idayat; 214
Hawke, Bob; 60, 97

Howard, John; 44
Ibeano, Professor Okey; 215
Ibrahim, Dr. Jibrin; 214
Ibrahim, Jibo ; 7
Ige, Bola; 38, 40, 211
Ikoro; 12
Imoudu, Pa Michael Aithokhaimien; 10, 55, 109, 126, 150
Itodo, Samson; 214
Iyang, Sunny; 136
Jackson, Reverend Jesse; 73, 107
Jakande, Governor Lateef; 29
Jean, Ping 166
Jega, Mahmoud; 34
Jibo, Dr; 215, 216
Jika, Abubakar; 34
Jinadu, Professsor Adele; 215
Johnson-Sirleaf, Ellen; 73
Jonathan, Vice President Goodluck; 129, 140, 144, 175, 187
Kagame, Paul; 93, 94
Kaltungo; 12
Kano, Aminu; 38, 55, 89, 129, 136
Kaunda, Kenneth; 48
Kawu, Modibo; 34
Ki-moon, Secretary-General Ban; 166
King, Martin Luther; 47, 122, 126
Kokori, Frank; 11, 179, 192
Kuguwai, Ntem; 5, 7
Kukah, Matthew Hassan; 161
Lafiaji, Shaba; 23
Lampley, Obetsebi; 73
Lawal, Muhammed; 136
Lawal, Muhammed; 23
Lumumba, Patrice; 99, 100
Machel, Gracia; 81
Machel, Samora; 126
Mahmud, Dr; 126
Makeba, Mariam; 79
Makhan, Vijay; 119
Mallam Ibrahim Nock; 12

Mandela, Nelson; 18, 26, 27, 36, 39, 47, 48, 56, 66-69, 75-77, 88, 89, 99-100, 105, 113, 116, 121-126, 145-148, 176, 181-183, 195-200, 203, 212
Mandela's moral challenge; 18
Manuel, Bob; 57, 203
Mao, Chairman; 10
Mark, David; 67, 83
Masa, Abdulrahman Black; 35, 36, 136
Masekela, Hugh; 79
Mbeki, Govan; 146, 198
Mbeki, Thabo; 147
Michael Imoudu Labour Institute; 23
Mongele, Dr Gertrude; 73
Moses, Adio; 11, 109
Mother Teresa; 126
Moume, Dr. Felix; 202
Movement for Progressive Nigeria (MPN); 9
Mpamugo, M.E.; 11, 109, 151
Mugabe, Robert; 48, 58-60, 77, 95-98
Muhammed Uwais; 214
Muhammed, Dr Bala; 57, 203
Muhammed, Murtala; 99, 117, 126, 129
Muhammed, Salisu; 179
Muktar, Dr. Mansur; 138
Musa, Balarabe; 38, 135, 155
Musa, Sultan Mansa; 39
Mustapha, Rauf; 7, 216
Muzeveni, Yoweri; 63, 145
Muzorewa, Abel; 51, 63, 97
Mwanawasa, Levi; 117
N'Dour, Youssou; 79
Nduka Eze; 12
NEPAD; 17
Nigeria Labour Congress (NLC); 10, 23, 109-116, 127, 142, 149-153, 177-179, 190-192, 202, 204-206, 210-213
Nkomo, Joshua; 48, 51, 63, 97
Nkrumah, Kwame; 5, 39, 47, 71, 72, 88, 89, 99, 126, 129, 199, 202
Nujoma, Sam; 46-48, 73
NUNS/NANS; 9, 112, 115
Nwabueze, Professor Ben; 201
Nyerere, Julius; 47, 48, 71, 99, 100, 158

Nzeribe, Gogo Chu; 11, 12, 109
Nzo, Alfred; 56, 203
Obama, Barack; 104-108, 129, 134, 154, 156, 158, 177, 200
Obasanjo, Olusegun; 29, 41, 45, 69, 73, 77, 81, 87, 91, 93, 141, 146, 161, 162, 165
Obi, Governor Peter; 143, 174-176, 199
Odah, Comrade John; 214
Odeyemi; 11
Odinkalu, Professor Chidi; 184
Ofori Atta, Williams; 73
Ogbonna, Armstrong; 11, 109, 179
Ojeli, Chief David; 135, 151
Ojukwu, Chief Emeka; 40, 131, 167-169, 174-176
Okadigbo, Chuba; 31
Okonjo-Iweala, Ngozi; 42
Olorode, Professor; 170
Olukotun, Ayo; 6
Omar, Abdulwaheed; 177, 204
Oni, Chief Segun; 167
Onimode, Professor Bade; 170
Onoge, Professor Omafume; 125
Osagie, Lawson; 179
Oshiomhole, Adams; 11, 38, 161, 177, 190-194
Oshuntokun, Professor Akintunde; 133
Osunde, Dr Lasisi; 109-116, 126
Oyerinde, Olaitan; 193, 194, 210-213
Oyo, Remi; 40
Ozo-Ezon, Dr Peter; 170
Pakenham, Thomas; 49, 61
Patriotic Youth Movement (PYMN); 9
Pohmaba, President Hifikepunye; 48
Political economy without Claude Ake; 14
Professor Jega; 214
Rafsanjani, Auwal Musa; 214
Ransome-Kuti, Beko; 126
Reagan, Ronald; 101-103
Rimi, Abubakar; 134-137
Rodney, Walter; 14, 36, 47, 49-51, 61-63, 126
Rufai, Ibrahim; 136
Ruth First; 14

Sambo, Namadi; 187, 188
Saraki, Dr. Abubakar Olusola; 21-24
Saul, John Paul; 102
Shagari, Alhaji Shehu; 141, 164, 176
Sharon, Aaron; 43
Siddique, Dr Abubakar; 214
Sisulu, Walter; 25, 26, 36, 75, 76, 146, 198, 199
Sithole, Ndabaningi; 51, 63
South West Africa People's Organization of Namibia (SWAPO); 46
Soyinka, Wole; 37-40, 75
Straw, Jack; 60, 96, 98
Sunmonu, Hassan; 11, 23, 135, 142, 149-153, 170, 192
Tambo, Oliver; 56, 125, 198, 199, 203
Tanimu, Yakubu; 214
Taylor, Charles; 63
Thatcher, Mrs Margaret; 103
Tongogara, Josiah; 97
Toure, Sekou; 99, 202
Tsavangirai; 96
Tukur, Dr. Mahmood; 5, 7, 49, 61
Turok, Professor Ben; 170, 173
Tutu, Desmond; 75, 198
Ubani, Chima; 52, 55
Uche Onu; 12
Ujudud, Sheriff; 34
Umar, Abubakar; 38, 40
UNDP; 10
Usman, Dr Yusuf Bala; 5, 6, 8, 49, 52-56, 61, 126, 170, 201
Usman, Hadiza Bala; 214
Wilmot, Patrick; 36
Xiaoping, Deng; 10
Yakowa, Patrick; 161, 187-189
Yakubu, Tanimu; 139
Yar'Adua, General Shehu Musa; 91-93
Yar'Adua, President Musa; 22, 83, 93, 128, 129, 138-144, 164-166, 187
Yau, YZ; 214
Yero, Muktar Ramalan; 188
Young, Andrew; 102
Yunus, Professor Muhammad; 123
Yusuf, Dadoo; 56

Yusuf, Mallam Kabiru; 214
Zuma, President Jacob; 122, 170
Zungur, Sa'ad; 55

www.ingramcontent.com/pod-product-compliance
Lightning Source LLC
Chambersburg PA
CBHW060035030426
42334CB00019B/2334

* 9 7 8 9 7 8 5 3 3 2 1 5 5 *